Liverpool Unitarians
Faith and Action

*Essays exploring the lives and contributions to society of notable figures
in Liverpool Unitarian history*

Edited by Daphne Roberts and David Steers

Cover design by Alison Steers

Printed by Trimprint Ltd., 36 English Street, Armagh BT61 7BE

Published 2014 by the Merseyside and District Missionary Association

ISBN 978-0-9929031-0-7

CONTENTS

Acknowledgments 1

Photographic credits 2

Introduction 3
David Steers

Memorials of the Ancient Chapel of Toxteth Park 7
Bernard Cliffe

Jeremiah Horrocks 1618 - 1641 27
Bernard Cliffe

William Roscoe 1753 - 1831 31
David Steers

A Short History of the Rathbone Family 39
Annette Butler

The Unitarian Family of George Holt 43
Bernard Cliffe

Noah Jones 1801 - 1861 55
Philip Waldron

James Martineau 1805 - 1900 61
Len W. Mooney

Joseph Blanco White 1775 - 1841 69
David Steers

Kitty Wilkinson 1786 - 1860 75
Daphne Roberts

John Johns 1801 - 1847 79
David Steers

William Henry Channing 1810 - 1884   85
Richard Merritt

Charles Pierre Melly 1829 - 1888   89
John Keggen

Sir Henry Tate 1819 - 1899   93
Richard Merritt

Sir John Brunner 1842 - 1919   97
Len W. Mooney

Lawrence Redfern 1888 - 1967   103
Elizabeth Alley

Sir Adrian Boult 1889 - 1983   109
Richard Merritt

The Visitors' Book of the Ancient Chapel   121
Bernard Cliffe

Contributors   127

Acknowledgments

Thanks goes to everyone who co-operated in the production of this volume but particularly to Daphne Roberts who conceived and began the whole project and who assembled the original selection of articles. I would like to extend my thanks to Mary Stewart and Alison Steers for their help with the digitization of some of the text and illustrations and to Annette Butler who was an invaluable aid in sourcing a number of images from the Liverpool Record Office. I am very much indebted to Phil Waldron who has taken many photographs for this volume and who tracked down a number of portraits for inclusion here which, to the best of my knowledge, have never been published before. A number of the illustrations used come from my own collection. Thank you also to all those who supplied photographs or made illustrations available and especially to Alison Steers who designed and produced our cover.

David Steers

Cover Illustrations

Front cover (clockwise from left): The Triumph of Truth, detail from the library ceiling of Ullet Road Church, painted by Gerald Moira (Photo: David Steers); The Good Samaritan Window, Gateacre Chapel (Photo: Philip Waldron); 1934 bronze representation of the *James*, the ship on which Richard Mather and the puritans sailed to Massachusetts in 1635, Ancient Chapel of Toxteth (Photo: Philip Waldron); front elevation of Ullet Road Church, 1899 (Photo: David Steers); detail of Liverpool Town Plan 1725 by J. Chadwick showing the original dock designed by Thomas Steers in 1709.

Back cover (clockwise from bottom left): Richard Mather; Kitty Wilkinson; Joseph Blanco White; William Rathbone V; James Martineau; Bronze relief panel depicting 'Charity' by J.H. Foley and T. Brock on the pedestal of the memorial to William Rathbone V, Sefton Park, Liverpool (Photo: David Steers).

Photographic credits

The full list of photographic credits is as follows:

p. 7 photo David Steers; p. 10 photo David Steers; p. 12 from H.D. Roberts *Hope Street* (Liverpool 1909); p. 17 Ancient Chapel, photo David Steers; p. 20 Ancient Chapel, photo David Steers; p. 21 Ancient Chapel, photo Philip Waldron; p. 24 Ancient Chapel, photo Philip Waldron; p. 27 Ancient Chapel, photo David Steers; p. 29 photo David Steers; p. 32 from a drawing by T. Hargreaves engraved by J. Thomson; p. 33 from a drawing by S. Austin, engraved by R. Wallis; p. 37 Ullet Road Church, photo David Steers; p. 40 Liverpool Record Office; p. 41 Liverpool Record Office; p. 44 Ancient Chapel, photo Philip Waldron; p. 45 photo David Steers; p. 47 Ancient Chapel, photo Philip Waldron; p. 51 Ancient Chapel, photo Philip Waldron; p. 53 Liverpool Record Office; p. 56 Gateacre Chapel, photo Philip Waldron; p. 59 Rivington Chapel, photo Philip Waldron; p. 60 from A.W. Jackson *James Martineau A Biography and Study* (London 1900); p. 62 from H.D. Roberts *Hope Street* (Liverpool 1909); p. 63 from a drawing by G. & C. Payne engraved by J. Smith; p. 66 from H.D. Roberts *Hope Street* (Liverpool 1909); p. 68 from an engraving by F.C. Lewis; p. 69 portrait by an unknown artist, Ullet Road Church, photo Sue Steers; p. 73 photo David Steers; p. 75 Liverpool Record Office; p. 77 photo David Steers; p.78 Gateacre Chapel, photo Philip Waldron; p. 80 Ullet Road Church, photo Philip Waldron; p. 83 Ullet Road Church, photo Philip Waldron; p. 84 lithograph by W.G. Herdman 1843; p. 85 Liverpool Record Office; p. 87 from Anne Holt *Walking Together* (London 1938); p. 88 lithograph by W.G. Herdman 1843; p. 90 Liverpool Record Office; p. 91 Ullet Road Church, photo Philip Waldron; p. 93 portrait by an unknown artist, Ullet Road Church, photo Philip Waldron; p. 95 Ullet Road Church, photo David Steers; p. 98 Ullet Road Church, photo Philip Waldron; p. 101 Liverpool Record Office; p. 103 from Alec Ellis (ed.) *Lawrence Redfern* (Bournemouth 1968); p. 105 from Anne Holt *Walking Together* (London 1938); p. 108 Ullet Road Church, photo David Steers; p. 110 Liverpool Record Office; p. 116 from H.D. Roberts *Hope Street* (Liverpool 1909); p. 118 from Emily Sharpe, *Pictures of Unitarian Churches* (London 1901); p. 122 photo David Steers; p. 124 photo Philip Waldron; p. 126 lithograph by W.G. Herdman 1843.

INTRODUCTION

David Steers

This book explores some aspects of the contribution to society made over time by selected members of the Unitarian community in Liverpool. The Unitarian church is a small but long established part of religious life and has always had a particularly prominent place in the life of Merseyside and district. Through biographical studies and examinations of particular families as well as a study of some of the historic monuments associated with them the various authors seek to draw out the part played by members of this particular community in areas of education, literature, social welfare, science, industry, commerce, the arts, theology and other aspects of life.

The story begins, appropriately enough, with the Ancient Chapel of Toxteth. One of the oldest non-conformist meeting houses in the country and the mother church, not just of Unitarianism on Merseyside, but really of all religious non-conformity in Liverpool. In a groundbreaking article Bernard Cliffe examines the rich heritage of monuments and memorials situated in the Chapel and its grounds some of which date back to the early seventeenth century. The Chapel predates the great ejection of 1662 by some decades having its origins in the puritan settlers who came to the former royal hunting forest of Toxteth Park to clear it and begin farming there when it was still a remote rural backwater. Unitarian theology developed only slowly and these early settlers would have held to a much more orthodox theological outlook, while possessing the same sense of independence of mind and determination of purpose that has characterized the Unitarian community throughout its history. In the next chapter Bernard draws out something further of the life and outlook of the Chapel in its early days under the ministry of Richard Mather through a discussion of the youthful scientific genius Jeremiah Horrocks.

By the end of the eighteenth century the puritan theology of the first dissenters in this community was starting to move towards a more rational and less dogmatic approach coloured by a greater curiosity about the world and the place of humanity in it. In no one was this new approach more apparent than in the person of William Roscoe, "Liverpool's greatest citizen" who possessed a vision of Liverpool as an Athens of the north and who so effectively opposed the slave trade despite its central place in the economic growth of the city and whose life is outlined by the present writer.

The contribution of some families from a Unitarian background has been particularly remarkable, sustained, as it has been, over many generations and in two chapters provided by Annette Butler and Bernard Cliffe we discuss the roles of the Rathbone and the Holt families in terms of both their contribution to the mercantile and commercial development of the city and to its social and charitable welfare.

Another later dynasty – who made a particularly important contribution to the development of Liverpool University – was that of the Jones family. They had their origins in Liverpool with the Rev Noah Jones, minister of Gateacre Chapel and an early proponent of a more radical Unitarian theology. His story is told by Philip Waldron.

The ranks of the ministry of the Unitarian church have contained some remarkable people and Len Mooney discusses James Martineau, perhaps the most prominent Unitarian theologian and thinker of the nineteenth century and someone who held a leading ministry in Liverpool.

One of the features of Liverpool life from the time of its emergence as a major port in the eighteenth century onwards has been its place at the centre of a nexus of international contacts. Many of the biographies in this book reflect this rich and diverse background which brought people to the city from across the British Isles and from around the world. So other stories show the Unitarian contribution to Liverpool life by people who came from Switzerland, Ireland, America and Spain. The present writer recounts the life of Joseph Blanco White whose long pilgrimage brought him initially from Catholic Seville to Anglican Oxford although it was not until he became a Unitarian in Liverpool that he found any theological contentment. Kitty Wilkinson was part of the waves of impoverished Irish immigrants who found their way to Liverpool and she was one of those whose own labours were bound up with making basic sanitation available to the most marginalized in society. Her story is told by Daphne Roberts. Another major Unitarian outreach to the poorest parts of society was the Domestic Mission movement – an idea which originated with Joseph Tuckerman in Boston. In Liverpool there were two Domestic Missions but the first one had as its missioner John Johns, a young west country poet who eventually sacrificed his life in serving his flock. An account of his life is given by the present writer. William Henry Channing was another prominent clergyman in the city who ministered to two Unitarian congregations in Liverpool but who was born in Baltimore and returned to the US to serve as Chaplain to the House of Representatives during the American Civil War. His story is told by Richard Merritt.

John Keggen tells us about Charles Pierre Melly who had Swiss antecedents but was also a member of a well-known Liverpool family whose own efforts towards the amelioration of the poorest members of society can still be seen today. With Sir Henry Tate and Sir John Brunner we have two of the most successful businessmen of the nineteenth century whose benefactions to the city and to the nation remain signally important. Fittingly the arms of the two men stand together above the fireplace in the hall of Ullet Road Church. Their biographies are provided by Richard Merritt and Len Mooney.

For subjects from the twentieth century we have an article by Elizabeth Alley on Lawrence Redfern, a beloved minister both before and after the Second World War and one of a number of distinguished ministers to serve the Unitarian church in Liverpool. Again representing the contribution of Unitarianism to culture and society Richard Merritt provides a biography of the leading conductor Sir Adrian Boult.

To conclude, the book returns to the Ancient Chapel with an examination by Bernard Cliffe of the Visitors' Book – something which so many churches and chapels possess but which is seldom scrutinized or examined.

A great many of the subjects in this volume can be found in the *Oxford Dictionary of National Biography*. What is different about these biographies is that the authors seek to place the individuals or families in the context of their faith. The spirit which motivated each of the families and individuals mentioned in the text was born out of their identity as members of their churches. What is also different about this book is that each chapter is contributed by an author who is part of the same story – by birth, by membership, by upbringing – members and ministers of the churches in Merseyside. Each biographical section also finishes with a short list of further reading containing the sources used and some other books which might be of interest.

This book is not intended to be hagiography but it does try to outline how one group of people – members of a particular faith community with deep historical roots but with an aversion to fixed creeds – were inspired to serve their fellows in different ways. Their legacy can be seen all over the city – in its parks, in its monuments, in the university, in hospitals, in education, in art galleries and museums - and it exists in the long and continuing struggle to create a society that gives equality and opportunity to all its citizens. It is not meant to be an exhaustive account of all the eminent members of the churches and chapels in the region. Readers will notice that the names mentioned are part of wider connections of family and business which extends to many others who could be included. There are other figures who could be the subject of such biographical accounts. But this is a selection of some of those who have followed the call of faith to be of service to wider society.

In 1931 the invitation to Ullet Road Church minister Lawrence Redfern to preach at a special service in Liverpool Cathedral caused, what was termed by some Anglican authorities, a "grave scandal" against the Church of England. In their letter of apology to Lawrence Redfern, Dean Dwelly and Canon Raven went to great lengths to repudiate this negative reaction and to acknowledge the contribution of Unitarians to Liverpool life. Listing many prominent members of the community by name (including many of the subjects of this book) they emphasized the service given to Liverpool by Unitarians. In *Walking Together*, written in 1938, Anne Holt, the historian of Liverpool Unitarianism, quotes at length the letter written by the Dean and Canon Raven. Perhaps a few lines of what they said might provide an appropriate final word for this introduction:

> To anyone who knows Liverpool it is obvious that…no one can interest himself in any effort to promote the religious and moral welfare of our City without discovering how vast is the debt which we owe to living members of the Unitarian churches. For ourselves we reckon our friendship with them as among the most precious gifts that our work has brought us, and we know from rich experience that to question their right to be called Christians would be for us a sin against truth and an outrage upon God.

Memorials of the Ancient Chapel
of Toxteth Park

*An examination of some of the monuments and gravestones in
Liverpool's oldest non-conformist chapel and grounds*

Bernard Cliffe

Names printed in bold type are to be found on memorials at the chapel

The Ancient Chapel of Toxteth stands at the end of Park Road, Liverpool, at its
junction with Dingle Lane, these names giving some clue to its rural past. The Park
had been a royal hunting park since the thirteenth century, but towards the end of
the reign of Queen Elizabeth I it became the property of the Earl of Derby, and
later of Sir Richard Molyneux, ancestor of the Earls of Sefton. At this time the
unoccupied parkland was settled by Puritans, who were attracted by its extra-
parochial status and by its isolated situation, perhaps an hour's walk from
Liverpool, then little more than a village. In 1611 they built a school for the
children of the twenty or so families then living in the area, and appointed the
fifteen-year old **Richard Mather** as the schoolmaster. With the encouragement of
the congregation Mather went up to Brasenose College in 1618 to continue his
studies, but after a few months the congregation invited him to return as their
minister. Although Richard Mather had not yet been ordained, he conducted the

The Ancient Chapel of Toxteth

7

first service in the newly built chapel before a large congregation, which included the Bishop of Chester, on 30th November 1618. Over the door of the chapel, in November 1918, a tablet was placed to celebrate this first service, and it seems remarkable that a congregation suffering from the devastating experience of the First World War should have had the will to undertake this work of commemoration. There is no memorial in the chapel to Richard Mather, but in the vestibule is a copy of his portrait, made near the end of his life by John Foster, and the original is thought to have been the first woodcut portrait to be made in the Massachusetts Bay colony.

By the 1770s the chapel was in a dangerous state of disrepair, so that, with the support of prominent dissenting ministers, **William Harding**, the minister, and the congregation made an appeal for subscriptions from the public. The appeal was signed by the minister and **John Rigby, Jonathan Mercer, William Lassell, Daniel Mather** and **John Houghton**, whose graves are to be found near the later south porch of the chapel. By their efforts the building was preserved, as the sum necessary was raised, and a substantial part of the upper walls and the roof were rebuilt. Over the centuries a number of changes have been made to the building, the largest of which was the demolition in 1841 of the school, seven years older than the chapel, and its replacement by the present porch and vestibule, so that the chapel gained largely the form in which we now see it.

Divisions among the Dissenters

Following the Restoration of 1660 there were two factions at the chapel, with two ministers, with each minister conducting the service on alternate Sundays. In spite of differences of opinion, there must have been tolerance, as the arrangement lasted through the shared ministries of the **Rev Thomas Crompton**, appointed as minister by Parliament, from 1656 to 1696, and the **Rev Michael Briscoe**, minister from 1662. After the passing of the Act of Indulgence of 1676 Michael Briscoe secured the necessary licence to preach at the chapel, and a copy of this document is to be seen in the vestry. Mr Briscoe served the Congregational faction at the chapel, while Mr Crompton was the leader of the Presbyterians. He too obtained a licence.

Many of the congregation were residents of Liverpool, who, with no chapel of their own, had made the Toxteth Chapel the focus of activity among dissenters of the district. In 1698 the Presbyterian section of the congregation of Toxteth Park Chapel decided to establish a chapel at Castle Hey, where the **Rev Christopher Richardson** and the **Rev Samuel Angier** became ministers. Both of these men had been jointly ministers at the Ancient Chapel, and continued in their work together serving the new congregation. It should be remembered that at this date the castle still stood. Castle Hey Chapel, the first dissenters' chapel in Liverpool, was the predecessor of Benn's Garden Chapel and Renshaw Street Chapel, the congregation of which moved to the new Ullet Road Church at the turn of the twentieth century.

In the latter part of the eighteenth century there were again divisions in the congregation of the Ancient Chapel. William Harding, minister from 1737 to 1776, was considered to be unconventional, and was Arian in his views. Mr Harding died on 15th July 1776 at the age of 85 after the restoration work on the chapel had been completed, and the **Rev Hugh Anderson** was appointed minister of the chapel. He was Unitarian, and this was too much for the more conventionally minded members of the congregation, the Independents, who left the Toxteth Park Chapel to set up a new chapel in Newington, which at that time stood in the fields outside the town, to be reached by a stile, and was regarded by some as inconveniently situated. Those who remained at Toxteth followed the leadership of Hugh Anderson, a Scot from Galloway, and since that time the congregation has been Unitarian.

Memorials at the Chapel

The names of all of the ministers of the chapel are displayed on a board in the east porch, and portraits of those who served in later years are placed on the walls of the two staircases. Some were buried at the Ancient Chapel, where their gravestones may be seen. The list of names begins with that of Richard Poyle, a Puritan minister who served the congregation before the building of the chapel, but his role is uncertain. There is some evidence to show that his ministry continued in the district after the opening of the Toxteth Park Chapel.

The chapel has a number of memorials, mostly from the eighteenth and nineteenth centuries, while the graveyard contains a large number of stones, the oldest that can be read dating from 1720.

Between the chapel and the meeting rooms, built in 1902 and extended in 1927, is a court, attractively laid out with flower beds. Steps lead from the courtyard to the slightly raised area of the New Ground, while the gates open directly onto the pavement of Park Road. The courtyard is paved in part with gravestones, but it is not clear where they had been sited before the court was laid out. One of these stones is a small slab to mark the site of four graves set aside for **the Herculaneum Pottery Benefit Society**. It is reasonable to suppose that this society was a burial club to which workers paid regular contributions. Some stones used in the construction of the court and pathway show that some earlier gravestones had been reused.

From the meeting rooms a door opens onto the court, dated 1934, the year of the opening of the first Mersey Tunnel. The decoration on the bronze doors includes a representation of a ship, *James*, the vessel in which Richard Mather and his family sailed in 1635 to join the Puritan settlement in Massachusetts. A tablet on the wall of the meeting room informs the visitor that the courtyard was laid out in 1934 as a memorial to **Henry Yates Thompson**, whose ancestors had worshipped at the chapel from the earliest times, and who was created a Freeman of the city in 1901. Henry Yates Thompson was related to **Richard Vaughan Yates**, and was a collector of rare books and manuscripts, a number of which passed after his death into the care of the British Museum. In his younger days he had visited the United States and Canada, where, through the means of family connections, he travelled widely, being present in November 1863, at the Battle of Chattanooga, conducted on the Union side by General Grant. An account of his experiences in America may be read at the Liverpool Record Office. In the Palm House of Sefton Park a stone tablet records his generosity in the building of this structure, now restored in a rather different form after the damage sustained during the Second World War.

The Arcade in the graveyard

The interior of the chapel is laid out in the style favoured by dissenting congregations of the seventeenth century. A broad arch, made after the demolition of the school in 1841, leads to the chapel from the vestibule and entrance porch. The focus of worship is the wooden pulpit of the late eighteenth century, which stands against the south wall, with a small table before it. The lower floor is fitted with box pews of late seventeenth century construction, the oldest bearing the carved lettering D M, and the date 1650, a reference to **Daniel Mather**. Against the outside of the east wall is a gravestone bearing the name of another **Daniel Mather**, who died in 1773. The noise of the traffic on the busy main road leading from the city to Aigburth, Garston and Speke, and on towards the bridge at Runcorn, is made less intrusive by the thick sandstone walls and the double glazing of the windows, although this is in an older style than today's visitors might recognize. The windows, with restrained decoration, on either side of the pulpit are themselves a memorial, placed by his parents, **Hugh** and **Evelyn,** to **Edward Reynolds Rathbone**, who died in an accident on 20th September 1913, at Crinnan, an event recorded on a brass tablet placed near the pulpit. The lower windows of the north side of the chapel have lettering inscribed by a number of individuals in the glass with initials and dates from the early years of the nineteenth century. In some instances these scratched words are beautifully done, and the visitor is left to ponder on the kind of opportunity taken by the perpetrators, but still there is a certain charm in all of this, and perhaps the building did not then command the same respect that it now enjoys.

A number of memorial tablets have been placed on the inside of the walls of the chapel. One of these records the life and greatest achievement of **Jeremiah Horrocks**, one of England's greatest astronomers. Few records of his life have been discovered, so that there has been some dispute about the facts of his birth, life and death, which occurred at the age of 22 years. The accounts that he wrote of his discoveries were published at the instigation of the Royal Society, but not until 1672, 31 years after his death, because of lack of funds. Much interest was shown in this memorial by visitors to the chapel in 2004, when his life was celebrated on the occasion of the transit of Venus, with great attention paid by the newspapers and television to the act of commemoration. Another transit occurred on 6th June 2012. The claim made on the memorial in the chapel that he was born in Toxteth Park seems in the light of modern research to be unjustified, and it is more likely that he was born in Bolton and was brought at an early age to Liverpool, where his family had connections with the Aspinwalls. A memorial to Horrocks was installed in the nearby church of St Michael in the Hamlet in 1826, and another in the church at Hoole in 1875. It was not until a petition was presented by a body of eminent scholars that a monument in his honour was erected in Westminster Abbey, close to the memorial of Isaac Newton, on the occasion of the transit of 1874. The observations of the transits led to better calculations of the distance between Sun and Earth.

In 1936 **Lawrence Hall** published in the *Transactions of the Historic Society of Lancashire and Cheshire* an account of the history of the Ancient Chapel, in which he wrote that for some years before its demolition in 1841 it had been the practice for burials to be carried out in the school next to the chapel, which had been built in 1611, and like the chapel itself, had undergone in the course of time some rebuilding. After the removal of the school building in 1841, two memorial stones which had been inside the school were placed in the porch of the new vestibule. One gives the names of members of **the Whiteside family**, while the other, placed on the right side of the doorway leading to the chapel, records the lives of members of **the Kennion family**. **Elizabeth Kennion** died in 1836, and hers is believed to have been the last burial to be carried out in the school. Her parents, **Peter Kennion** and **Elizabeth Walker**, lost two sons and three daughters in infancy, with Elizabeth the last surviving daughter.

The children's corner in the vestibule was furnished by **Mrs Winifred R. Rathbone** and her family as a memorial to **Herbert Reynolds Rathbone**, a former Lord Mayor of the city who died in 1930.

It had been customary in the early years for burials to take place in the chapel itself, and a number of gravestones are to be seen in the passageway which runs the length of the chapel. On the wall near the pulpit is an ornate tablet erected by members of **the Mather family** in the late nineteenth century. This refers to the nearby burial of members of the family, although nothing can be seen of these graves. It is possible that they are outside the building, where two others are to be seen, those of **Ann Mather** and of **Daniel Mather**. This tablet is presented in Old English lettering with Latin style dates, and is rather difficult to read. A brass tablet on the south wall refers to **Edward Aspinwall**, who died in 1656, and is thought to be the son of Edward Aspinwall who was the mentor of the young Richard Mather, and a leader of the first settlers. The brass tablet was set originally in the paving, but was removed in 1930 to prevent further wear. The chapel has a copy of the Journal of Richard Mather, taken from the internet and presented to us by a visitor to the chapel. It gives a vivid picture of his journey with his family from Liverpool to Bristol, telling of pirates, storms and near-shipwreck, and on to

Richard Mather

Massachusetts, in 1635. In the vestry is a picture of the church at Dorchester, Massachusetts, at which Mather was minister for many years until his death in 1669.

In the chapel floor, opposite the pulpit, is a small, irregular stone which records the death of **John Haven** on the ninth of May, 177-. The year of his death, 1773, was established only by reference to the history of the chapel written by the Rev Valentine D. Davis, who was minister from 1883 to 1894. In the chapel yard is the grave of **Martha Haven**, his widow, who died in 1797, and on this stone he is described Lieutenant John Haven, Royal Navy. As far as can be discovered he was the only officer of the Royal Navy to have been buried at the chapel. It is of interest to note the condition of the gravestone of Martha Haven, as it shows little sign of weathering, while the cut of the lettering remains sharp, and is in a remarkable state for a stone of its age. It seems reasonable to assume that John Haven was the last person to be buried in the chapel before the partial rebuilding of 1774.

Records held at the chapel include a register of burials, and a register of baptisms, kept at opposite ends of a single volume. There is also a grave register, begun in the mid-nineteenth century by **Philip Henry Holt**, and this shows the name of the proprietor and the names of those buried in each grave, a valuable source of information, as a considerable number of those who are buried have no memorial on the gravestones. The grave register is concerned only with graves in the New Ground, and we have no documents relating to the graves in the Old Ground. The entries in the burial register begin with that of William Briggs on 14th March 1785, while the baptismal register begins with the name of Henry Denton, on 6th January 1778. These registers were begun by the **Rev Hugh Anderson**, appointed in 1776 to succeed the **Rev William Harding**, but the volume now in the chapel is a copy made in 1856 by the minister, the Rev John Robberds, of the documents forwarded to the Non-Parochial Registers Commission at Somerset House. The copying must have been a long and laborious task, but the high quality of the handwriting remained constant. The **Rev Hugh Anderson's** records are often tantalisingly brief, with entries such as

Mr Ashton's child 23 January 1796 aged 4
Mr Freeland's child 21 March 1793 aged 7 months.

In some instances further information can be found on the gravestone, if one has been set up, but this is not always the case.

Hugh Anderson, too, wrote in a beautiful hand, as may be seen from a receipt he wrote for the sale of a plot, which has been preserved in the grave register. The question arises of why the receipt had not been given to the owner at the time it was written.

A marriage register, as distinct from the documents required by the Registrar-General for the conduct of weddings, was begun in the 1870s, with a small number of entries made retrospectively by the then minister. These records are invaluable in reading badly worn stones, often of sandstone, but the oldest stones were placed before the start of the registers we now have, and little can be done in such cases. Occasionally the information needed to read worn stones can be found in 'Epitaphs', the work of J. Gibson in the 1870s and 1880s. He recorded the epitaphs in non-conformist graveyards and chapels, and his beautifully written manuscript is kept in the City Record Office, but it is now available to readers on microfilm.

Some of the gravestones at the Ancient Chapel to which he refers have been removed or are now impossible to read.

The question arises of how permission was sought and granted for the placing by friends and family of the memorials inside the chapel, and which are still of such great interest to the visitor, but no record of this is known at present.

Epitaphs in the Graveyard

The graveyard is in two parts. The Old Ground, granted by Sir Richard Molyneux, lies close to the north and east walls of the chapel. In the early years of the nineteenth century an additional piece of land to the north of the Old Ground was bought from the Earl of Sefton by a lengthy and complicated process, which Lawrence Hall described in his history of the chapel, and it was not until after the death of the chapel secretary, **Richard Vaughan Yates**, that the New Ground was secured by the trustees. Between the Old Ground and the New Ground can be seen a line of stones which show the position of an earlier boundary wall. The additional land was needed because of the pressure during the early years of the nineteenth century on all burial grounds in the city. The non-conformist churches in the town had been built on small sites without graveyards, or they could accept no more burials, while the Old Ground at the Ancient Chapel, dating from the seventeenth century, was also becoming full. A gravestone in the New Ground bearing the name of **Walter Thomas** reveals that he was buried in the Necropolis, a commercial burial ground in Everton, and now a park, Grant's Gardens. There are no other names on this stone, but the Graves Register shows that three of his family were buried in the grave. When the New Ground was opened up grave plots could be bought by anyone, so that the people whose names are recorded were not necessarily members of the chapel congregation, nor even of other Unitarian congregations. There are several instances of the burials of Roman Catholics; one of these was that of **Giovanni Mozzara**, a seaman aged 31 from Genoa. The service was conducted at home by the parish priest, Father Dillon, KC, and there is no other record of him than the entries in the burial register and the grave register. It seems very sad for this young man to have died so far from his home and family. The trustees reserved a number of places for the burial of the poor, but the building of the Meeting Rooms in 1902 took up a large part of the unused land.

The memorials in the chapel and in the graveyard are of great interest, even though some of them carry only names and dates. One gravestone carries only a number, but an entry in the Grave Register reveals the names of the persons buried there. The burials in the New Ground took place in the nineteenth and early twentieth centuries, and readers will recognize the names of individuals and families who were prominent in the life of the city and beyond. Much has been written about many of these people, and it is enough here to recall their names, which were well known in their time, and down to the present day for their leadership in public affairs, in commerce, in education and in charitable effort. We read the names of members of the families **Booth, Boult, Brunner, Cook, Cox, Gair, Gaskell, Holland, Holt, Jevons, Lamport, Lassell, Meade-King, Melly, Oates, Rathbone, Roscoe, Swinton, Yates** and many others. The names often point to connections between families, and in some graves, particularly in the Old Ground, it seems to have been customary for wives to be identified by their maiden names, a great help in tracing family connections. Other memorials at the Ancient Chapel record the life and work of men and women who took a leading part in the work of Unitarians in the churches and in the domestic missions, and of many people whose achievements are not now so widely known.

It is fitting to recall the work done on behalf of the Ancient Chapel by three of its members, who, in addition to carrying on their business activities were able to give time to the duties of the offices they held at the chapel. **Richard Vaughan Yates** was the son of the **Rev John Yates**. He was senior partner in the firm of Yates, Cox and Cox, and was able to devote much of his energy and his wealth to his interest in education, municipal affairs and the improvement of the city. He was Secretary to the chapel, and it was during his time that the new land was bought for the chapel graveyard, although negotiations for the sale were not completed until after his death. His epitaph, which is in the Arcade, bears witness to the breadth of his vision, to his life of service to the people of the city, and to the respect and affection of his friends. It was through his efforts and generosity that the people of Liverpool enjoy access to Prince's Park, which lies close to the Ancient Chapel.

Richard Vaughan Yates was succeeded as Secretary of the chapel by **Philip Henry Holt**. He too was a businessman, a cotton broker and director of the shipping firm popularly known as the Blue Funnel Line, founded by his brother Alfred. He gave a good deal of his time to the affairs of the chapel, and he made it one of his first tasks to set up a new grave register, necessary to record the names of the proprietors of each grave, together with details of burials. Some of his remarks in the book indicate that he thought that perhaps affairs needed closer control. A few letters are preserved in the Grave Register, and they show his personal involvement in the management of the burial ground. He too was a man of great vision, with enormous concern for improving the condition of ordinary people of Liverpool. He was secretary of the chapel for over 40 years, a remarkable achievement recorded on his memorial in the chapel. In addition to the inscription in the Arcade, his friends have placed a memorial tablet in the chapel.

G. Kenneth Cook first held office at the Ancient Chapel in 1900 as secretary of the Recreative Society. He had been an outstanding student of accountancy, gaining first place in the examinations of 1902, and he set up in partnership as Cook and Leather, later to amalgamate with the firm of Harmood Banner and Son, from which he retired in 1955 as senior partner. During these years he continued to serve the chapel, becoming Treasurer in 1913, an office he held for fifty years. Members of his family continue to give invaluable support to the congregation in the management of the chapel.

Two other members of the congregation gave long service as organists at the chapel. **Mary Forester**, who died in September 1895, was organist for 25 years. **Joseph T. Ellerbeck**, who was born in 1808 and died in 1899, was organist for many years, and in 1858 the congregation marked their appreciation with the presentation to him of a silver salver. Recently a descendant wrote to the chapel seeking information about other members of the family, and sent a photograph of this piece of silver. Two of the gravestones record the lives of members of the Ellerbeck family.

At the Ancient Chapel there are memorials to a number of medical men, including **Dr Jardine, Dr William Reynolds, Dr Matthew Dobson, Dr Joseph Goldie and Alfred Higginson**, a prominent surgeon. In the paving by the north wall of the chapel is a gravestone bearing only the name of Matthew Dobson and the date 1779 and is perhaps the burial place of his daughter Elisa. Inside the chapel is a large tablet, unfortunately cracked, with a Latin inscription, a moving eulogy of Elisa. Matthew Dobson was a distinguished physician practising in Harrington Street, and at the time of the death of Elisa he held an appointment at the Liverpool Infirmary, situated on Shaw's Brow on the site now occupied by Saint George's Hall. He was born in Yorkshire in 1732, the son of the Rev Joshua Dobson, and gained his degree at Edinburgh University in 1756. During his time at the Liverpool Infirmary he attended several patients suffering from diabetes, and having carried out experiments he published his observations on the urine in these cases in 1776. He carried out other work on the study of atmospheric conditions and their effects on the body. His cultural interests were wide, and he wrote two chapters for Dr Enfield's *History of Liverpool*. He was elected FRS in 1778, the first Liverpool physician to be so honoured. He was also elected first President of the Liverpool Medical Library in 1779.

After the death of Elisa, Matthew's health began to fail, so that in 1780 he gave up his appointment and his practice, and with his wife Susanna left Liverpool to reside in Bath. Susanna was born Susanna Dawson, daughter of a London clergyman, and married Matthew in 1759. The couple had two other children. The eulogy to Elisa makes no mention of Susanna.

After they moved to Bath Susanna introduced her husband to her physician. Susanna, who has an entry in the *Oxford Dictionary of National Biography*, achieved distinction through her translations of French literary works, the most popular of which was *A History of the Troubadours*, which had passed through five editions by 1805, a considerable achievement.

While the couple lived in Bath Susanna aspired to joining the fashionable literary circle of Mrs Thrale, but she was given no encouragement, perhaps because of her reputed overbearing manner.

In 1784 Matthew died, and was buried at Walcott in Bath. Susanna died in London in 1795. It was thought that she was buried at St Paul's, Covent Garden, but there appears to be no evidence of this.

A translation of the inscription was made by the **Rev C.M. Wright**, minister of the Ancient Chapel from 1918 to 1928. It was a pleasing experience on one of the recent National Heritage weekends to find a boy of about fourteen, whose school included Latin in its curriculum, making a good attempt at his own translation. Presumably Matthew composed the Latin words, and would have been gratified to know that there would be some who would read them. The **Rev Charles Wright and his wife** have memorials in the chapel graveyard.

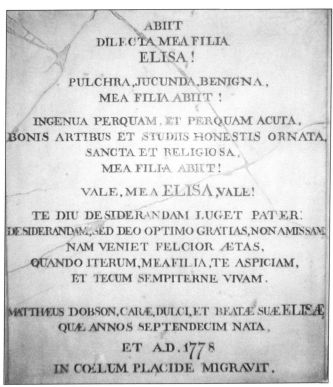

Memorial to Elisa Dobson

Joseph Goldie's name follows that of his wife, **G. Goldie**, who died on 14th May 1788, aged 43. It is unusual that she should be named in this way, with only the initial of her forename. Dr Goldie was born on 5th May 1741, and died on 3rd June 1825. His gravestone tells us that he was formerly the surgeon of the Eighth King's Own Regiment. There is an error here, as the Eighth Regiment was the King's

Regiment, later the King's Liverpool Regiment. After leaving the Army he became a surgeon in Liverpool, but enquiries about him at the Liverpool Medical Institute and at the office of the regiment failed to produce any information about his life. His military service would have been of great interest, as the British Army of the day served in many parts of the world. The newspaper obituary notice for the time of his death contained what was later inscribed on his gravestone, with the additional information that he had died at his home in Rodney Street. A search of the internet was more helpful about his family circumstances, through the website of the Gilchrist family. **Grizel Gilchrist** married **Joseph Goldie**, a surgeon working in Liverpool. Their families had long-standing connections through business and marriage, and lived in Dumfries, where James Gilchrist had been Baillie, as was Thomas Gilchrist in 1783. Many of the Gilchrist family had settled in America during the eighteenth century, as is related on their website.

Alfred Higginson is buried at Norwood, Surrey, but his name appears on the gravestone of his children. **Catherine** died 5th February, 1834, **Constance** died 16th November, 1844, aged 10 months, and **Frances Ellen** died 22nd September 1845 aged 3 years. Another daughter was Harriet Emily, who died in 1917, and lived in the Lake District. Their son was the Reverend Philip Martineau Higginson.

Alfred Higginson was born in 1808 and died in 1884. His wife Ellen, who died in 1878, was a sister of James and Harriet Martineau. Alfred was an eminent surgeon appointed to the Royal Southern Hospital in 1857, and remained consulting surgeon until his death. He also held an appointment at the Liverpool Children's Hospital. He designed a number of instruments which were widely used. Although he had made advances in surgery and was held in the highest regard, it seems that no obituary notice appeared in the medical press.

Nobody who reads the inscriptions can fail to be moved by the large number of very young children and young women whose deaths are recorded. It is a sad task to read of these family tragedies, and it should be remembered that these were children living for the most part in comfortable circumstances.

The Nuttall family lost five children, the oldest at the age of seven years.

In loving memory of
Robert aged 7 years
John aged 1 year and 3 months
Oliver aged 1 year and 4 months
Ada aged 1 year and 6 months
The beloved children of James and Elizabeth Nuttall
Also William Oliver aged 1 year and 3 months

It would seem from the cut of the lettering that the name of William Oliver was inscribed after the memorial had been put in place.

Agnes, daughter of John and Mary Currie
Died aged 17 months February 1872
Maud Mary her sister died May 1875
Mary Ann sister of Maud Mary
Born December 4 1879   Died December 6 1879

In memory of Ann Boyce Jevons
Infant Daughter of Frederick
And Sarah Acland Jevons
Born November 23rd, died November 26th 1868
The Lord hath given and the Lord hath taken away
Also their infant son
Died March 24ᵗʰ 1875 aged 2 days

Sacred to the memory of
The infant daughter of
George and Sarah Melly
Born and Died 26 August 1861

In affectionate remembrance of
Hedley Vicars Bowring
Born 31st July 1877, died 12th February 1878
Also of John Bowring
Father of the above
Died June 11th, 1888 aged 61
Also of Mary
Wife of the above John Bowring
Died November 1914, aged 77

In July 2002 Jane and Scott Bowring, then living in Exeter, visited the chapel to see this grave, and later wrote to express their appreciation.

Sacred to the memory of John Hughes
Who died 16th December 1858 aged 69 years
Also to Ann, wife of John Carmichael
And daughter of the above
Who died 10th January 1860, aged 35 years.
Also to John, son of Ann Carmichael
Who died January, 1860, aged 2 weeks
Also to Mary, granddaughter of the above John Hughes,
Who died aged 2 years

Also to Jane Ann Carmichael
Who died September 1862 aged 2 years

There are on the gravestones many such memorials to mothers and children, reminding us of the high mortality rates of the nineteenth century.

Inside the chapel is a tablet placed to the memory of **Hugh Pringle**, who died in September 1775 aged 7 years, and his sister, **Ursilla Ann**, who died at the age of six years in September 1777. The parents were **Hugh** and **Ursilla**. Hugh's death at the age of 63 in 1784 is recorded but there is no further mention of Ursilla, the mother of the children. In a different style of lettering is the record of the death of Hugh's widow, **Dorothy Pringle** on 14th November 1804 at the age of 79.

James Hornby died aged 55 years in 1809, while his widow **Margaret** died in 1830 at the age of 76. Their daughter Ann died in 1795 aged 2 years, and their son Daniel died in 1800 aged 3 years.

The daughters of **David** and **Mary Shaw** were **Margaret**, who died at the age of 18 years in 1827, **Ann**, the eldest, who died in 1828 at the age of 21, and **Mary**, who died aged 21 in 1829. It must have been a devastating experience for all of the family to endure such a terrible and rapid succession of events.

HUGH PRINGLE Son of
HUGH and URSILLA PRINGLE
born the 27th of August 1718
died September 8th 1755.

URSILLA ANN, Daughter of
HUGH and URSILLA PRINGLE
born June 20th 1751.
died September 18th 1757,
HUGH PRINGLE Esq.
Ob: 15th August 1784 Æt: 63.
Also Dorothy his Relict
Who died, Nov. 14. 1804.
Aged 79. —

Memorial to Hugh and Ursilla Pringle

In memory of Sarah Avison, wife of Thomas Avison
Of Liverpool, Attorney at Law,
Who died 2nd of April 1803 aged 33 years
Also of Joshua, the infant son of
The above Thomas Avison and Sarah Avison.
Also of Susannah Avison, daughter of
The above Thomas and Sarah Avison
Who died 6th October 1837 aged 36 years.
Also of Jane Jones, the faithful servant
Of the above Susannah Avison.

Faithful Servants

It is touching to read the name of **Jane Jones** on the gravestone of the Avison family, and their expression of appreciation of the service she had rendered. Two other families have expressed their gratitude in the same way.

The memorial to the **Rev Robert Lewin**, who died in January 1828, for nearly half a century minister to the congregation of Benn's Garden Chapel, bears the name of **Mary Flanders**, the family's faithful servant for more than fifty years. The last name on this memorial is that of **Frances Ann Lewin**, who died at Birkdale in 1924, and is interred at the chapel.

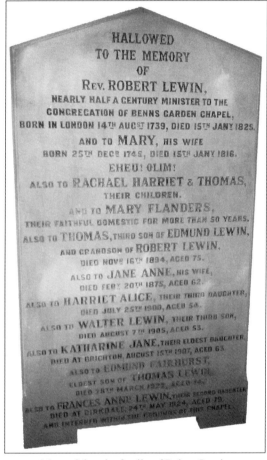

Memorial to the family of Robert Lewin

Jonathan Hobson died in 1833, and his wife **Mary Taylor** in 1845, aged 79. **Mary Malkin**, faithful servant of Mary, died in 1844 at the age of 72. This gravestone is one of those forming part of the paving in the court.

Mary Hodge, daughter of **William Ronan Hodge** died aged 17 on 11th September 1811, only one month after the death of her father.

In the family of **Edward Flower**, his daughter **Emma** died at the age of 13 years in 1843, while her sister **Mary** died in 1848 at the age of 18. **Mary Ann**, the wife of Edward's eldest son died at the age of 24.

Some of the gravestones bear the names of family members who have died while travelling or working abroad.

Basil Rathbone, the son of **Richard** and **Hannah Mary Rathbone** was born on 5th April 1824, and died at Auckland, New Zealand, on 24th February 1853.

Wilfred Jevons, the second son of **Henry** and **Susan Jevons**, died at Arling, Wyoming, USA, on 17th February 1895, aged 36.

Arthur Fletcher, aged 23 years, died near Cincinnati, USA, on 17th January 1871.

Edgar William Harvey, aged 22, died at Featherstone, New Zealand, on 15th October 1876.

John Harvey, aged 23 years, died on the passage to Ceylon on 2nd August 1861, and was buried at sea.

Charles Scott Simpson was buried at sea 7th January 1907.

George Simpson was lost at sea in September 1878.

Robert Nicholson died at sea on 19th October, 1785, aged 20.

Samuel Nicholson of the same family died in Jamaica on 9th June 1804 aged 33 years.

There are in the graveyard memorials to **Joseph King** and his family, and to **Richard Horwood**, both of whom were leaders in their field. There is continued interest in their work which can be readily seen in a perusal of the internet. Joseph King, who died in 1822, aged 72, was an accountant, and in his epitaph he is described "as the compiler of the well-known King's Interest Tables", which were used in the calculation of compound interest. His book was greatly valued by practitioners, and was reprinted as late as the 1890s. A copy was in 2009 offered for sale on the internet, presumably as a collector's piece.

Joseph King's death was reported in the *Liverpool Mercury* of 27th December 1822 "On Friday last, Mr Joseph King, Islington, aged 73".

Richard Horwood died in 1803, and the inscription tells in a rather cramped style of his achievement.

Sacred to the memory of Rd
Horwood, who, with great Ingenuity
And Indefatigable Industry
Designed and executed the celebrated
Plans of London and Liverpool.
He died October 2nd 1803.

His plans were street plans made as a commercial venture, and when complete his London plan was on a scale of 1:2400, covering most of the land in London that was then built up. It was intended to show every house with its street number, which at that time was a relatively new idea, having been introduced in the

1730s. To undertake his work he needed to raise capital by enrolling subscribers, among whom were the King, local authorities, insurance companies and landowners, all with a need for accurate and well-drawn plans of the streets. In spite of this support his work was hampered by shortage of funds. He himself did almost all the work of the survey, and may have supervised the engraving, a task which took a considerable time, during which his backers saw no return for their investment. He had to deal with some landowners who would not allow him onto their land to survey the off-street areas. After working on his London map he came to Liverpool, which was expanding rapidly, and produced a map in six sheets which he dedicated to "the Mayor, Bayliffs and Common Council of Liverpool". He was still beset by money difficulties, and died a poor man at the early age of 45, having done much to improve the quality of maps. There was no plan equal in quality to his map of London until the middle of the nineteenth century.

Horwood's maps still attract interest. They are being published again with marginal contemporary embellishments, as he had intended, but was not able to carry out. The firm offering this service does so on the internet.

Inside the chapel is a memorial tablet to **George Perry**. The grandson of a Lord Mayor of London, George Perry was born in 1719 in Somerset, and died in Liverpool on 3rd February, 1771, aged 52. He had been sent to be apprenticed as a clerk at the Coalbrookdale Ironworks, but he soon demonstrated his practical skills. He was later sent by the managers to set up a small warehouse in Liverpool in the street now named York Street, and there Perry began to work on projects of his own, and travelled the district to market the articles his company made, visiting fairs, markets and isolated farms. One article which sold particularly well was an iron cooking pot. He expanded the business, and started to make equipment for the sugar industry of the West Indies. George Perry was a man of tremendous energy and wide vision. He was a patron of the Liverpool Library, assisted in the production of a map of the town, and proposed the construction of waterways between London and Bristol, and between Liverpool and Hull. He married **Lydia Ann Lacroix**, daughter of **Peter Lacroix**, a descendant of Huguenot refugees. His foundry stood in Lydia Ann Street. The foundry has gone, but the street named after his wife remains. After his death his firm was managed by Joseph Rathbone, and later became the engineering business Fawcett, Preston and Company. An informative book on the two hundred year history of this great company was published with the title '*Fossetts*', a copy of which may be seen at the Liverpool Record Office.

Few of the memorials make mention of the working life of the deceased. The gravestone of the family of **Swinton Boult** is informative. He was "The Founder, and for nearly forty years, the manager of the Liverpool, London and Globe Insurance Company". He died in July 1876, and was survived by his son Frederick.

Several schoolmasters are commemorated in the graveyard. **John Ashton** of the Hope School, Liverpool died in December 1802 at the age of 63, while the lives of **James** and **Elizabeth Ashton** of Harrington School are also recorded.

William Hartshorn, MA of Trinity College, Dublin, died in 1847. He was a master at the Liverpool Institute, and his memorial was raised by old friends and pupils, "In grateful remembrance by old friends and pupils to whom his memory is forever green."

The grave of William Hartshorn

A memorial "Erected by his former pupils and friends as a token of their love and esteem," pays tribute to **William Dugdale**, lately master of the Warrington School of Liverpool. He died on 3rd July 1776.

Major William Howe Greene, OBE, FRIBA, died in June 1937, and is buried with others of his family.

It is likely that those given the rank of Captain were mariners, as army officers would be known by their regiments, but **John Olive**, who died at the age of 80 in July 1877, may be clearly identified, as he served for many years with the Peninsula and Orient Company.

Mary Ann Caldwell, of Ombersley in Worcestershire, died in 1870, her name appearing in the burial register also. She was survived by her husband, **John**, of whose death there is no record other than the gravestone inscription, "died suddenly at his work, Chapel Street," with an incomplete date in 1898.

Killed in Action

The Ancient Chapel has no War Memorial, but some families have inscribed names on the gravestones of family members.

Major John Ashton Critchley, MC of Strathcona's Light Horse (RC) died of wounds on 1st April, 1917 in his 25th year. He was buried at Bray sur Somme, France. He was a grandson of William Durning Holt Senior.

Lieutenant Reginald Ernest Melly, 20th King's Liverpool Regiment. Killed in action near Guillemont, Battle of the Somme. 30th July 1916, aged 20.

Captain Arnold Richard Rathbone, fourth son of Benson Rathbone, died of wounds in France 24th June 1915, aged 52. Buried at Le Treport. (Captain Rathbone had been an officer in the Territorial Army before the war.)

Lieutenant George Benson Rathbone, RGA. Grandson of Benson Rathbone. Died in hospital in Bonn 28th May 1919.

Captain Cecil Heywood Brunner, RFA, 57 West Lancashire RAC Born 1873 died of wounds 1917. Buried at Doxinghem near Poperinghe, Belgium. He was a magistrate in Liverpool. (The name of Captain Brunner appears also on a memorial tablet in Saint Anne's Church, Aigburth.)

Roscoe Johnson, born 17th February 1889, died in France 12th October 1916. His father, John Johnson, died 6th April 1917

Per Ardua ad Astra. Flying Officer John Bernard Thompson Born 20th October 1922. Killed in action in France 19th July 1944

Other than the brass memorial to Edward Aspinwall there is no trace of burials from the time of the Puritan founders of the chapel.

This research has been a moving experience. The inscriptions, whether only a bare statement of name and date, or a moving message, or perhaps intended to impress also have a great deal to tell about our predecessors at the Ancient Chapel. The visitor, resting in the calm of the Ancient Chapel, or strolling in the chapel yard, is often left to ponder.

Further Reading

The material for this essay has been gathered from many sources, but chiefly from:

Valentine D Davies, *Some Account of The Ancient Chapel of Toxteth Park* (1884).

S.B. Gaythorpe, FRAS, *Transactions of the Historic Society of Lancashire and Cheshire*, 106, (1954), 23-33

Lawrence Hall, 'Toxteth Park Chapel in the 17th century', *Transactions of the Unitarian Historical Society*, 5:4 (1934) 351-383

Horace White, *'Fossets' – A Record of Two Centuries of Engineering* (Bromborough, Fawcet Preston & Co. 1958)

James Gibson, James Gibson's Liverpool Epitaphs (Computer File): Monumental Inscriptions – Liverpool (Liverpool & SW Lancs F.H.S. 2007) CD-ROM

Henry Smithers, *Liverpool, its Commerce, Statistics & Institutions with a History of Liverpool* (Thos. Kaye, 1825)

Lawrence Hall, 'The Ancient Chapel of Toxteth Park and Toxteth School', *Transactions of the Historic Society of Lancashire and Cheshire*, vol. 87 (1936)

An Everyday History of Liverpool, two volumes, (Liverpool, Scouse Press, 1981)

The Liverpool Medical Institute made notes available on Matthew Dobson.

JEREMIAH HORROCKS 1618 – 1641

Observer of the transit of Venus

Bernard Cliffe

In 2004 and again in 2012 the Ancient Chapel of Toxteth drew quite a number of visitors on the occasion of the two latest transits of Venus, an event which will not recur for one hundred and twenty years, a curious cycle of astronomical events. I think that few of our visitors came out of informed curiosity but it was very pleasing that so many were interested sufficiently to make the journey, and perhaps leave having learnt a little; that Horrocks was one of England's greatest astronomers, a scientist whose genius is ranked very highly and his memorial is set up in Westminster Abbey close to that of Newton; that his work on the planet Venus enabled a more accurate calculation to be made of the solar distance, the distance between Earth and Sun, one of the fundamentals of the study of the solar system; that his learning and scientific achievement were a triumph of will over not very favourable family circumstances, and perhaps chronic poor health; that we can never know the loss that all the world suffered as a result of his death at the early age of twenty-two.

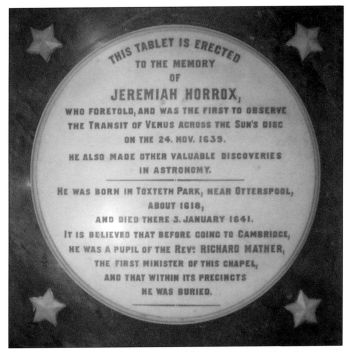

The Jeremiah Horrocks memorial in the Ancient Chapel

They may also have taken up the notion that scientific progress depends on establishing facts, and that the information about him displayed on the memorial in the Ancient Chapel has had to be revised in the light of recent painstaking historical research. They may also have realized that some things do not change much, and that Horrock's work was published by the Royal Society only after some considerable delay because of lack of funding. An account of the life of the boy and the young man has to be a matter of conjecture, with the generous use of qualifying words. It is significant that the earlier settlers in Toxteth Park, who had gone there in the hope of living undisturbed, saw fit to take care of the education of their children before they saw to the building of the chapel. It seems likely that the twenty or so families could gather for worship in one of the larger houses, or perhaps in the school, or, in fine weather, in the open. The style of the seating of the chapel, popular among dissenters at that time, could put the people in mind of a gathering around the preacher under a tree (the pulpit), with the congregation standing around. But not in the notoriously cold winters of the seventeenth century. Box pews were built to give some warmth.

Education in Toxteth Park

The choice of Richard Mather as schoolmaster at the age of fifteen would have been a matter calling for much deliberation. It appears that Richard Mather was concerned about the treatment of his charges. He himself had found that the atmosphere at the school at Winwick was uncongenial, to such an extent that his father intervened with the master on behalf of Richard.

We know little about the running of the school or its curriculum. Almost certainly the lessons would have involved the three Rs, and reading of the Bible. Printed books were becoming more within the reach of ordinary people and consequently it is believed that there was an improvement in the rates of literacy over the years. The supply of books for children was very limited, with few produced for children. It is likely that many of the people passed their entire lives without encountering any other book than the Bible, and it was with this that some of them learned to read.

Richard Mather, the minister would have recognized very quickly that Jeremiah was quite exceptional, and perhaps did his best to meet his needs. Not only did students need to be good readers, but also to have good, retentive memories, and good deductive powers. The making of notes cannot have been easy as writing was a slow business in view of the materials to hand. The poor lighting provided by candles must in winter have been a drawback. In earlier days even the supply of notepaper could sometimes be a problem.

A Victorian image of the Ancient Chapel

We cannot tell at what age Jeremiah learned to read and write in Latin, the language of the academic world, which has its place in the rituals of the older universities, but is important still in its own right as a field of study. Even in the 1950s, if not later, Latin was a requirement for admission to some Arts faculties. James Horrocks was fairly prosperous, but Jeremiah went up to Cambridge as a sizar, a college servant, in a tradition of the student working his way through college which continues to the present.

At some point he became interested in astronomy, the study of which was becoming of greater importance. Certainly there was opposition from the church of Rome, as Galileo found to his cost. There were few books on the subject, and of course older books had lost credibility. Horrocks managed to read what was there, and to him astronomy became of the greatest importance. His reading and his writing were all in Latin. For his observation of the transit of Venus he had to devise and make his own equipment.

He was rightly described as a genius. His greatness was at last recognized by the nation when the Council of the Royal Astronomical Society drew up a petition before the transit of 1874, signed by many famous men. The Dean and Chapter of Westminster Abbey accepted the petition, and an inscription was made.

In memory of
Jeremiah Horrocks
Curate of Hoole in Lancashire
Who died on the 3rd of January
In or near his 22nd year
Having in so short a life
Detected the long inequality in the mean
Motion of Jupiter and Saturn
Discovered the orbit of the moon to be an ellipse
Determined the motion of the lunar apse
Suggested the physical cause of its revolution
And predicted from his own observation the transit
Of Venus which was seen by himself and his friend
William Crabtree on Sunday the 24th of November (O.S.) 1639
This tablet facing the monument of Newton was raised after
The lapse of more than two centuries. December 9, 1874

Over the top of the monument are the words alluding to his having to leave his observation:

Allis temporibus ad majora avocatus quaea ob haec paserga negligi non decuit

Further Reading

The Records of the life of Jeremiah Horrocks

Few written records have been discovered, and details may be found in the paper written by S.B. Gaythorpe, FRAS, and published in the *Transactions of the Historic Society of Lancashire and Cheshire*, 106, (1954), 23-33. An unpublished paper by F.R. Burrell contains much detailed information.

The date of birth can be estimated from the recorded date of his matriculation at Emmanuel College, Cambridge, on 5th July 1632, and the best-informed deduction gives the date of his birth as on or about 4th January 1618.

The date of his death was noted by his friend William Crabtree as having occurred on 3rd January 1641.

The burial of his father, James Horrocks, is recorded as 4th March 1641.

No record has been discovered at the Ancient Chapel of the birth or death of Jeremiah Horrocks.

WILLIAM ROSCOE 1753 – 1831

Liverpool's greatest citizen

David Steers

In what used to be called Liverpool Museum on William Brown Street there was for many years an exhibition featuring the history of the city. One small section of this considered the contribution of Unitarians to the life of the city and alongside a large blown up picture of the Ancient Chapel of Toxteth was a display concerning William Roscoe. This quoted some words written about him by Washington Irving. He said of Roscoe:

> Wherever you go in Liverpool you perceive traces of his footsteps in all that is elegant and liberal.

Washington Irving was a prolific and popular American writer, the author of such well known stories as the *Legend of Sleepy Hollow* and *Rip van Winkle* and for a while served in the US diplomatic corps in England. Late in Roscoe's life Irving wrote in awe struck tones of his first meeting with him in the Athenaeum club:

> He had a noble Roman style of countenance; a head that would have pleased a painter; and though some slight furrows on his brow showed that wasting thought had been busy there, yet his eye still beamed with the fire of a poetic soul. There was something in his whole appearance that indicated a being of a different order from the bustling race around him. (Washington Irving, *The Sketch Book of Geoffrey Crayon, Gent.*, vol. 1, (Philadelphia 1829), 27, 24.)

Such rich praise was common for Roscoe in the nineteenth century. After his death an impressive memorial was erected in Renshaw Street Chapel, his youngest son published a two volume biography of his father, and on the centenary of his birth in 1853 a medal was struck in his honour. As the twentieth century progressed this sense of wonder at Roscoe's personality and achievements gradually diminished. Although impressive biographies continued to be published the positive quotation of the 1970s Liverpool museum gave way to a more guarded appreciation in subsequent Museums in Liverpool and whilst he continues to be honoured amongst Unitarians at least, the academic community seems less impressed. The hefty volume *Liverpool 800: Culture, Character and History*, published to mark the 800th anniversary of the city's charter and edited by John Belchem, gives only minimal notice to the man who in 1953 was still regarded as "Liverpool's greatest citizen". Whilst the adulatory excesses of two hundred years ago may well have been a potential source of embarassment to the great man himself the more recent slightly dismissive attitude based as it is on changing political and social agendas does not do justice to Roscoe's contribution to his home town.

Birth and background

By any standards Roscoe was a truly remarkable man. In the circumstances of his birth he enjoyed few material advantages. He was born on 8th March 1753 and grew up at the Bowling Green Inn at Mount Pleasant. His father had worked as a butler but was an inn-keeper and market gardener by the time of his birth. Today Mount Pleasant is a fairly unremarkable city centre street but in Roscoe's day it was a semi-rural area on the outskirts of the town.

William Roscoe

Although not wealthy people, Roscoe's parents must have given great encouragement to their son. From his father Roscoe inherited a tremendous energy and a lifelong interest in agriculture, gardening, and botany and from his mother he inherited a love of books and poetry. The site of the Bowling Green Inn gave Roscoe an impressive view of the growing city, including the docks and the many ships sailing in and out of the Mersey. A contemporary watercolour of this view, executed when Roscoe was 16, can be seen in the Walker Art Gallery. (Michael Angelo Rooker (1746-1801), *Liverpool from the Bowling Green 1769*).

The city was expanding rapidly as its importance as a trading and mercantile centre grew, considerable extra impetus being given to its expansion by war with France. Naval conflict with the French on the high seas gave ship owners the chance to make a fast profit through privateering. By fitting out their ships for warfare they sailed off in search of French merchant ships to attack and plunder which they did most successfully. In 1778 Liverpool privateers captured the French merchant ship *Carnatic* which had a cargo of diamonds and spices worth at that time an astonishing £135,000. But even the exploits of privateering began to be dwarfed by the money to be made from the purchase of slaves, known euphemistically as the African trade.

It was into this environment that Roscoe was born. But he was not marked out for greatness. He left school at 12 and went to assist his father in the market garden. Business was good but Roscoe did not allow his own education to cease.

He fell in with a like-minded group of young people and with them began to learn Latin, Greek, French and Italian. He developed too an interest in art and in poetry and was serious about the study of the New Testament.

He left the market garden at 16 to become articled to a local solicitor for a period of five years. He also further developed his studies when the minister of his church, William Enfield, left to be the rector of the Warrington Academy, attending open meetings there which extended his knowledge and, an important thing for dissenters of his time, gave him an appreciation of rational enquiry.

The house on Mount Pleasant where William Roscoe was born

In 1774 Roscoe qualified as an attorney and for the next twenty years worked in that profession, one which he did not particularly enjoy. And yet this might have been his lot in life, a respectable – although to him tedious – profession bringing in sufficient income to live quite well. However, Roscoe's talents, interests and beliefs meant that his life was to expand in a number of different directions.

Artistic and literary interests

Roscoe developed extensive artistic and literary interests. At a very young age in 1773 he was instrumental in setting up a Society of Encouragement of the Arts, Painting and Design, the first such society outside of London. His first published poem, written when he was only 19, was named after the place he lived, *Mount Pleasant*, and extolled the city's rise as a port to a place of international renown as well as delighted in the views of unspoiled countryside across the river on the Wirral and in North Wales.

But early on he developed an interest in the European Renaissance, particularly in the rise of the arts and learning in fourteenth century Florence. Although he never travelled to Italy friends brought him back from Florence books and other material for him to study. In 1796 he published his *Life of Lorenzo de Medici*. Medici was a great patron of the arts at the time of the early development of commerce and capitalism in Florence but Roscoe's book, when it was published, was met with critical acclaim and went into many editions while being translated into many different languages. This – together with his subsequent books, most notably the four volume *Life and Pontificate of Leo X* - was a remarkable achievement from someone who hardly ever left his home town and certainly never made the journey to Italy.

But his interest in the Renaissance also had a more practical purpose for Roscoe. He began to see himself in the same light as Lorenzo de Medici, doing for Liverpool what Medici had done for Florence, that is developing the cultural aspect of a growing city in the throws of enormous change. Roscoe began a large and important collection of paintings, manuscripts and books. His success in his working life gave him the resources to do this. Indeed so successful was he in his business life that he was able to retire from his legal work at the age of 43.

But although he retired from his chosen profession he was too much of a public minded figure to retire from public life or from public activity. He moved to Allerton Hall, the same house where his father had once worked as a butler before William was born. In this rural area he took up farming, he also continued his writing and political campaigning.

Opponent of the slave trade

From the very start he had been an opponent of the slave trade. His poem *Mount Pleasant* had included an indictment of slavery and those who profited from it:

> Torn from each joy that crown'd their native soil,
> No sweet reflections mitigate their toil;
> From morn, to eve, by rigorous hands opprest,
> Dull fly their hours, of every hope unblest.
> Till, broke with labour, helpless, and forlorn,
> From their weak grasp the lingering morsel torn…
> Till Death, in kindness, from the tortur'd breast
>   Calls the free spirit to the realms of rest.
>
> Shame to Mankind! But shame to BRITONS most,
> Who all the sweets of Liberty can boast;
> Yet, deaf to every human claim, deny
> That bliss to others, which themselves enjoy.

A few years later he went into print with a longer poem, published in two volumes, and entitled *The Wrongs of Africa* which brought him wide fame and established him as a leader of the abolitionist cause. He devoted all the income from this publication to the London Committee for the Abolition of the Slave Trade and followed it up with a prose attack on the trade, *A General View of the African Slave Trade, demonstrating its Injustice and Impolicy*.

To do this required no little moral courage. To publicly make such statements was to go against the tide of public opinion as well as question the means of acquiring wealth of so many of his fellow citizens, some of whom sat with him in church every Sunday. His attack on slavery was rebutted by the City Council who paid a clergyman to write a theological rebuttal of Roscoe's arguments. Yet he was inspired by his faith to oppose this trade, he was encouraged by his friend and former minister the Rev William Enfield, and felt a great impetus towards standing up for what he knew was right because of his reflections. Amongst his poetry he began also to write hymns which were popular in their day, contributing many to a new hymnbook for his church.

His opposition to the slave trade brought him into the political arena and in 1806 he was encouraged to stand for Parliament as an independent candidate. This was a difficult and stormy campaign. His opponents – the 'Church and King party' – identified his religion as the root cause of his opposition to 'the African trade'. One squib spoke sarcastically of Roscoe the "staunch Presbyterian" who "will exert his utmost power to procure you that, so much desired object, the abolition of the African trade! Which has for so many years impoverished the town, and almost starved the inhabitants of Liverpool. Away with that unprofitable traffic. Roscoe and the Presbyterian interest for ever, huzza."

Another Tory tract was more direct:

> If this trade is abolished, what will become of yourselves, your wives and families? The answer is plain. You may beg your bread, or quit your country, for you will never obtain relief from Presbyterians. Now you all know Mr R----- and his party to be of that persuasion, the decided enemies of the African trade, and it is to assist his friends in abolishing this great trade, that he wishes to get a seat in parliament. (Quoted in Anne Holt, *Walking Together*, 158.)

But this identification of the town's dissenters with the home of abolitionist opinion was a result only of the hard work of Roscoe in the preceding years. Roscoe's family were members of Benn's Garden Chapel which moved to Renshaw Street in 1811 (and later to Ullet Road in 1899). But we should be cautious of assuming that all the forebears of modern Unitarians automatically shared in Roscoe's enlightened attitude towards the slave trade. In fact the opposite is the case. In the mid eighteenth century there were at least a dozen members of Roscoe's Chapel who were slave ship owners, that is active practitioners in the slave trade. On top of that the Chapel would have been crowded with sailmakers, coopers, ropemakers, chandlers and merchants of many kinds all of whom were deeply and actively involved in the slave trade in some form or other. When Roscoe raised his voice against the African trade he offended not only the religious and political establishment of the town but also many of his fellow dissenters. Yet against all the odds Roscoe was successful. Becoming an MP meant a rare trip away from Liverpool for Roscoe but he was able to go to the House of Commons where he spoke and voted in favour of the abolition of the slave trade. Telling the House:

> I have long resided in the town of Liverpool: for thirty years I have never ceased to condemn this inhuman traffic: and I consider it the greatest happiness of my life to lift up my voice on this occasion against it, with the friends of justice and humanity.

Of Roscoe the leading anti-slave trade campaigner, William Wilberforce, said: "Here is a man who by strength of character has risen above the deep-seated prejudices of his townspeople and eventually won their respect." (Quoted in Donald A. Macnaughton, 'William Roscoe', *Oxford Dictionary of National Biography*, Oxford 2004).

But he received little thanks in his home town. On his return to Liverpool he was met with a riot orchestrated by some of the local slave traders and he remained in Parliament for just about a year, until the next election.

But this is not the most important thing. He had achieved what he set out to do. An opponent of the slave trade he had been successful in bringing about its end. He was one of that group of people who were not cowed by the prevailing situation which took for granted the order of things but instead determinedly opposed what was wrong. Inspired by his faith Roscoe, like Wilberforce and others, could see that God could not intend any people to be kept in a state of slavery.

Roscoe was a man of complete integrity. His interests were wide and deep. A few years after he had retired from the law his friend William Clarke came to him for help. He was a banker whose business was in deep trouble. But Clarke had been the first person to bring back valuable manuscripts for Roscoe from Italy. Roscoe did not want or need to become involved in banking, but he did to help his friend, becoming a partner in his bank, and in doing so became a great success.

This lasted for a number of years. However, in 1816 the bank collapsed in a period of acute economic depression following the end of the wars with Napoleon. Roscoe was forced into bankruptcy and had to sell off his beloved home as well as his books, manuscripts and collection of pictures. This was a devastating experience for him, he particularly regretted the loss of his books although his friends purchased his valuable art collection and presented them to the Royal Institution, an educational institution which Roscoe had established in the town as a precursor to a University. Eventually this significant collection passed into the hands of the city and can today be seen in the Walker Art Gallery.

Gradually Roscoe's fortunes began to improve following his bankruptcy. He continued to write poetry and was made a member of the Royal Society of Literature in 1819, being given a royal payment of 300 guineas per annum in recognition of his services to literature.

Roscoe also wrote poems for children, of which the most famous is *The Butterfly's Ball and the Grasshopper's Feast* (1807) which proved to be a best seller and which continues to be in print. Part of his intention in such works was to get children to look at nature and enjoy all its features. This was an aspect of Roscoe's own great interest in nature and botany which found such fulfilment in his establishment of the Botanic Gardens in his home town, obtaining exotic plants from all over the world and helping to identify and classify them, publishing a botanical work *Monandrian Plants and the Order Scitamineae*, over the years 1824 to 1828.

Roscoe died on 27th June 1831, his wife Jane having died in 1824. They were married for 43 years and together had ten children. In later life Roscoe moved to the old lodge at the end of Lodge Lane. He became a member of the Ancient Chapel of Toxteth and is amongst the list of signatories to the call of the Rev John Porter as minister there in 1827, perhaps one of his last public acts before the debilitating strokes he suffered in that year.

Today Roscoe's portrait, featuring his "noble Roman style of countenance" still hangs in a prominent place in the Walker Art Gallery. In it he sits surrounded by tokens of his extensive interests and attainments. He was a man of extraordinary gifts and talents which he used all for good. Roscoe was

Memorial by J. Gibson to William Roscoe in the cloisters, Ullet Road Church

inspired by a vision of a city transformed, a city which was undergoing tremendous changes in his lifetime and which based its prosperity on a vicious trade. Yet he was not afraid to challenge this situation and ultimately was successful in helping to end the slave trade. Alongside this he held to a belief that Liverpool could attain great heights as a centre of cultural endeavour, as Graham Murphy observes he "nurtured the hope that Liverpool…would one day be as a beautiful a city as Florence." (*William Roscoe. His Early Ideals and Influence*, 30). While this could never be precisely achieved amidst the endless industrial and mercantile expansion of the nineteenth century he truly laid the foundation for the flowering of the city's cultural, educational and intellectual life. Without Roscoe and his circle it is hard to imagine that just over 200 years after they had helped to abolish the slave trade this city might even be considered as the European City of Culture.

Further Reading

Graham Murphy, *William Roscoe. His Early Ideals and Influence*, (Liverpool 1981)

George Chandler, *William Roscoe of Liverpool* (London 1953)

Donald A. Macnaughton, *Roscoe of Liverpool: His Life Writings and Treasures 1753-1831* (Birkenhead 1996)

Arline Wilson, *William Roscoe: Commerce and Culture* (Liverpool 2008)

Anne Holt, *Walking Together: A Study in Liverpool Non-conformity 1688-1938*, (London 1938)

A SHORT HISTORY OF THE RATHBONE FAMILY

From the Society of Friends to the Unitarians

Annette Butler

This chapter covers the period 1742 to the present day, and follows the progress of a truly remarkable family over two and a half centuries. 1742 is the year when first records of Rathbones involved in business in Liverpool appear. The timber trade brought the family to the emerging city's river Mersey and the opportunities provided, the Rathbones having originated in Gawsworth, near Macclesfield, Cheshire.

The second William Rathbone was the real entrepreneur. In the archives of what is now Rathbone Bros. Plc a daybook of 1742-47 records that William employed twelve sawyers. Ship owning and merchanting quickly expanded the family firm to many more employees.

The family were Quakers, membership of the Society of Friends gave a world network of honest trading contacts: a considerable advantage in both the long and short term. Such trustworthy links led to the company importing the first bale of cotton from the USA in 1784. (200 years later this was symbolically re-enacted in the Liverpool of 1984). Nearly 60 years on from first contact with the USA - in 1841 - the firm took on an Agency with the East India Co. which lasted until 1912.

Abolitionists

William Rathbone III was an early abolitionist, to the extent of refusing to sell timber to slave-ship owners. Both he and his son, yet another William, were amongst the first eighteen members of the Liverpool branch of the Society for Abolition of the Slave Trade. William Rathbone IV was one of only two Liverpool people brave and determined enough to sign the petition for abolition. Such political views and involvement in the Friends of Freedom anti-slavery group invoked hate mail and derision.

Spectacular growth in the cotton trade brought wealth and importance to the port of Liverpool, and William IV built a substantial house, 'Greenbank,' in leafy Mossley Hill (now in the ownership of Liverpool University).

Marrying into the Greg family

William IV was criticized by his co-religionists, the Quakers, for publishing a pamphlet about their activities in Ireland. His response was to leave the Society of

Friends. His son William Rathbone V, had a particular reason to do so, when he married 'out' to a daughter of the wealthy Greg family, owners of the cotton mill at Styal in Cheshire, who were significant Unitarians. The elder William was re-admitted to the Quakers, but later joined the Unitarians, where typical Rathbone liberal sympathies best found expression.

What Quakers and Unitarians and, indeed, other non-conformist adherents did share in common was a belief that if you were successful in business and/or had been born wealthy (the former the more likely route for wealth) then you were morally obliged to put something back into society: by campaigning for better conditions for poorer strata of society, and through practical philanthropy. This could take the form of anti-slavery agitation, prison reform, a little later on campaigning for slightly shorter hours/safer working conditions in manufacturing, and health provision.

William Rathbone V

William Rathbone VI (1819-1902) was to become the Rathbone family member most associated with health innovations and other remarkable improvements in ordinary, often very poor person's lives. Also, unusually in the long saga of the Rathbone family's influence, he was to produce a remarkable daughter rather than son, i.e. Eleanor Rathbone (of whom, more later). He is now best known for championing the new idea of District Nursing, following on from the family admiration and financial support of Kitty Wilkinson, whose pioneering practical work in her home area of the slum courts for cholera victims inspired the creation of the first ever Public Wash Houses (1842). This William continued his parent's support for the Liverpool Domestic Mission (founded in 1836 by Unitarians with support from ministers such as John Johns and John Hamilton Thom – the latter marrying Hannah Mary Rathbone). An interest in further education developed in the 1870s into personal funding and fund-raising from other successful businessmen to create University College of Liverpool (opened 1881). Interest in nursing occupied more than half his life, and his second wife (mother of Eleanor) employed the first school nurse in Liverpool. William also succeeded (with others) in gaining better conditions in workhouses. Following the death of his first wife in 1859, he vowed to establish a District Nursing system in her memory, with the support of his late wife's nursing attendant, "to go into one of the poorest districts of Liverpool and try, in nursing the poor, to relieve suffering and to teach the rules of health and comfort". Like many others, he corresponded with Florence Nightingale on nursing strategies, and implemented her views on eliminating the 'not respectable' image of nursing by proper training with qualifications. From 1863 the Liverpool Training School and Home adjoining the Royal Infirmary, Ashton Street and its enlargement in the 1870s was paid for by William himself and later by the family firm. Its great success inspired other cities to copy the rather radical idea. He also became an MP.

Eleanor Rathbone

The seventh generation of Rathbones saw the 'baton of public service' being handed on for the first time to a *female*, who never married. Eleanor Rathbone (1872 – 1946) was able to take advantage of the University education now opening to women. After gaining her degree Eleanor helped to establish the School of Social Science in 1905, where she lectured in public administration (and was an abiding inspiration to a young sociology student who later became the well-known Lady Margaret Simey). A University building, theatre and Chair of Sociology all honour her memory. Following the family tradition of being as usefully busy as possible, Eleanor, after Oxford, returned to Liverpool, a "whole hearted feminist", supporting the Suffragette Movement, during the First World War set up the Town Hall Soldiers' and Sailors' Families Organization, and in 1919 became leader of the National Union of Women's Suffrage Societies, and becoming an independent MP in 1929 until her death in 1946. She was also Liverpool's first woman councillor, representing Granby Ward from 1909-1934. She probably deserves on the national scale to be best remembered for her long campaign to introduce a

Family Allowance to be paid to the woman of the household. This was achieved by the Family Allowance Act of 1945, the year before her death. Eleanor also realized early on how dangerous the Hitler movement was, and campaigned on behalf of those fleeing from Nazi (and other Eastern European) persecution to the UK. She achieved a great deal for many people. In 2008 Eleanor Rathbone was honoured as 'Campaigner for Family Allowances' in a "Pioneering Women" commemorative set of stamps.

In summary (from the website of Rathbone plc): "from 1742 …Cotton

Eleanor Rathbone

trading and all such was abandoned in favour of becoming Financial Managers. In 1988 Rathbone Brothers merged with Comprehensive Financial Services to form Rathbone plc, thereby securing listing on Stock Exchange, remaining (in 2010) in the FTSE 250 Listed companies, managing £13 billions of Assets. As a wholly family concern and now corporately, Rathbones has always practiced practical philanthropy and built a formidable endowment. Present-day staff are encouraged to maintain links with the wider community."

Further Reading

Sheila Marriner, *Rathbones of Liverpool: 1845-73* (Liverpool University Press 1961).

Lucie Nottingham, *Rathbone Brothers: from merchant to banker 1742-1992* (London, Rathbone Bros. 1992).

Susan Pedersen, *Eleanor Rathbone and The Politics of Conscience* (Yale University Press 2004).

A huge archive of Rathbone papers is held in Liverpool University's Special Collections and Archives. Also online: Liverpool University Archives Hub (http://archiveshub.ac.uk/features/dec07.shtml)

THE UNITARIAN FAMILY OF GEORGE HOLT

Ship owners, engineers, railway pioneers, philanthropists

Bernard Cliffe

On 26th October 1937, Sir Richard Durning Holt, Bart., JP, took part in a ceremony held at the Holt High School in Childwall. The school and distinguished guests had gathered for the unveiling by Sir Richard of a memorial stone placed to mark the opening of the new building, which had been built to replace the older building in Bagot Street, in which the school had been established in 1907. The occasion was reported in the *Liverpool Daily Post*, and a brief account appeared in the school magazine in December 1937.

Sir Richard acknowledged the honour done to his family, and expressed his view that the school had been named with special regard to the memory of his uncle, Philip Henry Holt, who had done a great deal for education in the city. He said,

> My grandfather, who came to Liverpool as a comparatively poor boy, and made a fortune here, was early associated with the Mechanics' Institute, and he subscribed to the laying of the foundation stone in 1835. He was also concerned in the establishment of Blackburne House, the girls' school attached to the Institute.

He went on to mention the efforts of his uncles in the matter of public education, and for the continuing need for all people, irrespective of their backgrounds, to be given the opportunity to achieve their best. He used a very apt metaphor, *There is room for only one captain in the ship, but the others of the crew are supremely valuable*.

Arrival in Liverpool

George Holt, grandfather of Sir Richard, was born in Rochdale in 1790, the son of Oliver Holt, a merchant of woollen cloth, who had learnt his trade in Halifax. Oliver had had little education, and gave his son George the best that he could provide, with early days spent at a dame school, and later in the care of Dr Fawcett. Oliver was given his name as reminder of his great namesake of the seventeenth century, and of the proud non-conformist traditions of his forebears. George, at the age of seventeen, with, it is said, a guinea in his pocket, and perhaps a letter of introduction, set off to seek his fortune in Liverpool, where he was to succeed brilliantly. Given his family background, it was natural for him to turn to the trade in cotton, which was expanding rapidly. He became apprenticed to Mr Samuel Hope, and after his five year apprenticeship was ended he was offered, and accepted, a partnership. In 1823 the partnership was dissolved, and George Holt set up in business for himself, naming his firm George Holt and Company. On the dissolution of the partnership Mr Hope took over the banking side of the business, while George Holt took over the cotton brokerage, and, in spite of the ebb and flow of trade, his company flourished.

George Holt began to take an active part in the public affairs of the city. He was elected to the Town Council, in which he became a prominent figure over many years. During his time on the council he served on the Libraries Committee and on the Docks Committee. In his business life he was a man of vision. Dissatisfied with what he considered to be excessive charges of the London banks and insurance companies, he was instrumental with others in the setting up of the Bank of Liverpool, and in 1836 he took part in the establishment of the Liverpool Fire and Life Insurance Company, which eventually became part of the Liverpool, London and Globe Insurance Company. In the Chapel yard is the grave of Swinton Boult, who was for forty years the managing director of this company, while for many years Alfred Holt was a director of the company. Another venture which George Holt undertook was the construction of the first India Buildings, which was to house for many years his own offices and later those of the Blue Funnel Line. In 1924 the work began on the present building

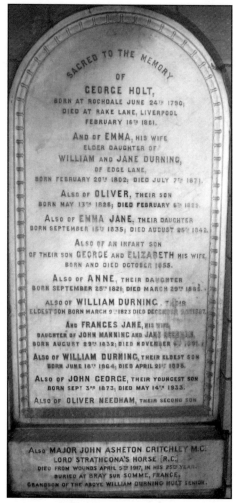

The Holt family memorial
at the Ancient Chapel

in Water Street, intended to replace the old, much smaller office building. Commissioned by the Blue Funnel Line, and designed by Herbert J. Rowse, this building was completed in 1932 at a cost of one and a quarter million pounds. India Buildings was damaged by bombing in the Second World War, but has been restored to its former splendour.

George Holt became acquainted with the Durnings, a wealthy and well-established family with a house in Edge Lane, which lay at that time in the countryside. The family owned land in the area, and from them George rented a cottage in Rake Lane, then at the edge of the town, and now called Durning Road. He was introduced to Emma, the daughter of William and Jane Durning. They married and made the cottage their family home throughout their marriage. George and Emma had two daughters and five sons, but Oliver died at the age of two years, and their last child, Emma Jane, died at the age of six. The other children went on to find fulfilling roles in their lives. The first child was Anne, who died unmarried in 1885 and wrote a history of the Durning family, the manuscript of which is in the care of the Liverpool Record Office. The first son was William Durning Holt, born in 1823, who married Frances Jane Needham, whose family are commemorated in the name of Needham Road, together with Holt Road and Durning Road, which lie between Kensington and Wavertree Road. The second son was George Holt, born in 1824, and who married Elizabeth Bright, daughter of Samuel and Elizabeth Bright. Oliver was born in 1826 and died in 1829. Alfred was born in 1829. He was married twice, first in 1865 to Catherine Long of Knutsford, at the Unitarian Chapel. Catherine died in 1869, and in 1871 Alfred married again, to Frances Long, the cousin of his first wife. In 1878 the couple moved to a new home, Crofton, in Sudley Road, Aigburth.

Philip Henry was born in 1830, and died in 1914. His wife, Anna Booth, died in 1899. The youngest son of George and Emma was Robert Durning Holt, who was born in 1832 and died in 1908, and who was destined to become the first holder of the office of Lord Mayor of Liverpool. In 1867 Robert Durning Holt married Lawrenciana Potter, who was one of nine sisters, one of whom, Beatrice, married Sydney Webb. On 14th October 1904, the Honorary Freedom of the City was conferred upon Robert Durning Holt.

The nineteenth century was a time of great change for the people of Liverpool, with a rapid

Holt's Arcade, India Buildings

45

expansion of the city beyond its boundaries. Trade was flourishing, and one of the most important commodities to be traded was cotton, King Cotton, as it was often called, so that it was possible for energetic and enterprising men to make considerable profits in the business, as George Holt had done, and so William and Robert entered the firm of George Holt and Company, where they were given a good training in all aspects of the cotton trade, and went on in time to take over the conduct of the business that their father had established. For short periods Alfred and Philip worked in the family firm, and this experience stood them in good stead in their own business ventures. Trade also required efficient transport, and it was in that direction that George, Alfred and Philip looked.

George became an apprentice with the well-established firm of T & J Brocklebank. At that time apprenticeship was the customary first step on the ladder for a young man who wished to make his way in business. The practice of premium apprenticeship existed whereby a fee was paid to the employer, who undertook the training needed by the aspiring craftsman or businessman. Such a system existed even in the twentieth century in some industries, now, perhaps, to be replaced by the greater opportunities for University education. It was not unusual for young men to begin their working lives on the shop floor of the firm owned by the parent or other relative, and, if they were perceptive, this may have given them some understanding of the lives and attitudes of the workforce.

On 1st October 1838 the first iron ship to be built in Liverpool was launched by Messrs Jackson, Gordon and Co. This vessel of 264 tons was named *Ironsides*.

Lamport and Holt

In 1845 George joined William James Lamport to set up the firm of Lamport and Holt. W. J. Lamport had learned the business of shipping in the office of Gibbs, Bright and Co. The partners built up a fleet of ships trading with Central and South America. At that time many ships were still built of timber, and were driven by the wind. Early steam ships often used their engines only as a supplement to the sails. The ships were small, with limited bunker capacity, the engines were not efficient, and the amount of coal needed was enormous, and expensive, so much so that at first only relatively short voyages were undertaken by steam alone, but the battle between the iron steamer and the wooden ship driven by wind power was under way. It is of interest to note that some shipping lines included the word *steamship* in the company name, an indication of the forward-looking outlook of the management, and, it was hoped, of the reliability of their vessels. The first steamship that the Lamport and Holt Company owned was *Zulu*, a vessel of 278 tons, built in Quebec. She was followed by a number of steamships, so that, following several amalgamations with smaller companies, Lamport and Holt became the principal line of steamers trading with South America, ordering ships that were built to meet the requirements of the trade. The company adopted the practice of naming their ships after famous men of science and the arts. Over the years Lamport and Holt sought to extend the field of their operations, and dropped any business that was not profitable, as was the case with trade in the eastern Mediterranean. They supplied troopships for the transport of troops and horses to the Crimea. The two world wars brought a flurry of activity for the company, and some losses. In the First World War one ship alone, the *Archimedes*, made 467 trips between England and France, ferrying 145,000 troops, together with large numbers of horses and other supplies required by the Army. The company acquired special vessels for the transport of animals, including some for horses needed in the South African war, and iron ships to transport coffee from South America to the United States, although some believed that coffee travelled best in wooden ships. For a time it held a contract with the Government of Brazil to maintain a coastal passenger service using vessels of shallow draught. Lamport and Holt were the first shipping line to carry frozen meat from Argentina to the United Kingdom.

W.J. Lamport was the son of a Unitarian minister of Lancaster. He took a prominent part in advising on the regulations which were the basis of the bill introduced in Parliament by Samuel Plimsoll intended to improve the safety of ships. W.J. Lamport and George Holt were business partners and friends, and both were Unitarians. George Holt's grave is in the Arcade of the Ancient Chapel yard, while that of William James Lamport lies a few yards down the path. He died a bachelor at his home in New Brighton.

The grave of W.J. Lamport at the Ancient Chapel

Alfred Holt began a lifelong engagement with steam power when he was at school. Passing through Knutsford, George Holt had come across a small school, Heathfield, conducted by Mr Green, a Unitarian. He placed his son in the care of the master, and Alfred appears to have found the regime congenial. As he grew older he was placed with Mr Cameron, an exacting master who drew the best from his charges, and this met with the approval of Alfred, himself a stickler for attention to detail. While he was at the school he was allowed to handle a working model steam engine, and it might seem to us now that the journey of his life was then laid out before him.

He was essentially an engineer. He was elected a member of the Institute of Civil Engineers, and he was elected president of the Liverpool Engineering Society, from whose *Transactions* much can be discovered about the achievements of Alfred Holt. But before all that was to follow, Alfred had to serve his time in the railway yards at Edge Hill Station. He started work in 1846 in the railway workshops of the Liverpool and Manchester Railway, apprenticed to Edward Wood, a highly qualified engineer, and attended evening classes in mathematics and other relevant subjects. He worked on locomotives and rolling stock, and was allowed to take charge of the construction of a number of bridges between Liverpool and Huyton on the line of the Liverpool and Manchester Railway. When his apprenticeship was complete there was a slack time in trade, and his father invited Alfred to join the family business. Instead, in 1852 he set up on his own account as a consulting engineer, with offices in India Buildings. Commissions were hard to come by, but he was engaged by Thomas Ainsworth to look at the problems of the *Alpha,* a small ship of unusual construction, part timber and part iron, and was able to put the vessel into working order.

Blue Funnel Line

This success encouraged him to buy another ship, his first, in need of attention, the *Dumbarton Youth*. At this time he met Captain Isaac Middleton, whose advice he valued, and who was to remain a lifelong friend. In addition to needing a large scale refit, this vessel lacked a funnel. This was ordered and assembled, but needed a coat of paint. The story is that in the storeroom of the ship was a plentiful supply of blue paint, which was used to cover the new funnel, and so Alfred Holt's later ships were known world-wide as the Blue Funnel Line.

At this time the shipping industry was developing rapidly, with steam not yet dominating the scene. There was dispute over the merits of the paddle steamer and the screw-driven ships, and the merits of the timber ship and the iron ship, later the steel ship, and as so often has been the case, it was the bold and far-sighted ship owner who first embraced the new technology, but,

> *Be not the first by whom the new are tried,*
> *Nor yet the last to lay the old aside.*

was a thought that many businessmen may have had in mind in the turbulent times of expansion in the nineteenth century.

It was this world into which Lamport and Holt, and later Alfred Holt plunged. A number of shipping ventures were tried. The need for shipping fell away after the end of the Crimean War, and operators had to seek new business opportunities. Philip joined Lamport and Holt for a while, and this company and Alfred joined in the trade with Central America, operating a service between the United Kingdom and Colon, where goods could be trans-shipped by the Panama railway. Alfred travelled with the first sailing on the new route. Competition was intense, and after a time Alfred sold out to a competitor, realizing enough to pay off his investors with a generous dividend.

In 1865 Alfred and Philip became partners to set up a new company, the Ocean Steamship Company, to become known world-wide by its popular name, the Blue Funnel Line, and which continued trading, with amalgamations, into the twentieth century. They had decided to develop a business with India, China and Japan, which was to benefit shortly afterwards from the opening of the Suez Canal, saving thousands of miles of sailing round the Cape of Good Hope. They commissioned three new ships, *Agamemnon*, *Ajax* and *Achilles* built to Alfred's design, and fitted with a new type of boiler which Alfred had designed to work at higher pressure, and so obtain greater fuel efficiency. Inefficient use of coal was costly to owners, requiring the vessels to have very large bunkers, which reduced cargo capacity, and the availability of bunkering facilities along the route. The new ships were a great success, and business prospered. *Agamemnon* made the first voyage under the command of Captain Middleton, for whom Alfred continued to have great regard. It is a coincidence worthy of note that at the Battle of the River Plate which took place in 1939, the Royal Naval ships in the engagement with the German *Graf Spee* were *Exeter*, *Ajax* and *Achilles*. The action brought about the scuttling in the River Plate of the German pocket battleship which had preyed on British merchant shipping in the same waters that Lamport and Holt ships had navigated in their trade with Argentina.

While the remarkable new steamships of Alfred and Philip Holt were trading with the Far East, there was still competition from sail. The clippers were beautiful ships of American design, intended for fast journeys, so that the fastest ship would be first in the market with the new season's harvest of tea. Their voyages aroused great public interest, with races between vessels over the thousands of miles ending on occasion with arrival times that were only a matter of hours apart. Clipper ships also operated on other routes.

Alfred Holt followed the example of his father in the matter of insurance. He believed that rates were too high and decided that the company's ships would sail without insurance, as the company was strong enough to bear any losses, and his aim always was to sail safe and reliable vessels. The Blue Funnel ships enjoyed a splendid reputation for their quality, and it was said of the high standard of management of the line,

So highly is its service valued, that among officers, engineers and sailors it is regarded as good fortune to become connected with the firm.

Shortly after this decision over insurance was taken, three ships were lost in a single year, but the policy was not changed. The Second World War brought heavy losses, with four hundred seamen lost, and fifty-nine ships sunk.

A reading of *An Everyday History of Liverpool*, a chronicle of events in the city over the centuries, published by the Scouse Press in two volumes, will show the alarming number of marine accidents that took place in the nineteenth century in the River Mersey, with other losses in more distant waters.

Liverpool Overhead Railway

Alfred was always in the forefront of public affairs, and was a member of the Mersey Docks and Harbour Board from 1867, becoming Chairman in 1891. He resigned the following year over a disagreement about a dock rebuilding scheme which he felt unable to support. His mind was ever active, and one of his concerns was the difficulty of travel along the line of docks, which were close to his office, and the waste of time and money that this involved. He had often travelled, and had visited New York, where he had seen the Elevated Railway. He saw that a similar structure would solve the problems of dockside travel. He drew up plans of all aspects of the proposed undertaking, down to the smallest detail, and worked out the likely cost. Eventually the proposal was adopted, and the Liverpool Overhead Railway, the only one of its kind in Great Britain, was opened, and served the city well for many years until the 1950s. At the formal opening of the railway on 4th February 1893, in the presence of a distinguished assembly, Lord Salisbury and others paid tribute to him as the originator of the new engineering wonder. Alfred Holt had first presented his idea to a meeting of the Liverpool Engineering Society. The first section of the Overhead Railway, from Herculaneum Dock to Alexandra Dock was not opened to the public until 6th March 1893, while the final extension to Dingle was completed on 21st December 1896. The railway closed on 30th December 1956. The disused platform of the Dingle station now serves as a motor car repair shop, reached by a ramp which is big enough to have been used by wagons.

Another of his ideas, which was not adopted, was the laying of a plateway between the Liverpool docks and the cotton towns of east Lancashire, which he believed would improve their competitive position. His plan was to design vehicles which would operate on a metal track, but without the flanged wheels of the railway, so being capable of using ordinary road surfaces. This he believed would reduce handling costs. He drew plans, and worked out costs, but the idea did not find support.

He retired from active management in the company, but continued to maintain an interest, and he visited the company office in India Buildings on the day before he died. Visitors to the Ancient Chapel graveyard may have wondered why his name does not appear on the family memorials, on which can be read the names of so many of the family. Alfred Holt was an early advocate of cremation, and so it was with his funeral, when his cremation took place with a private service at Anfield Crematorium.

Philip Henry Holt spent almost all of his working life as the partner of his brother Alfred in the management of the Ocean Steamship Company, the Blue Funnel Line. He also was the secretary of the Ancient Chapel, in which office he succeeded Richard Vaughan Yates. One of the first actions he took on taking up the office was to establish in 1861 a Grave Register, as distinct from the burial register which had been started by the Rev Hugh Anderson in 1785. The first date recorded on the Grave Register is that of the burial of Philip's father, George Holt, in 1861. Perhaps it was this event which had prompted thoughts of opening such a register. Philip Holt left a note in the book indicating that he wished to establish a rather tighter control over this matter, in order to prevent disputes over ownership and mistaken identification of graves. The grave register recorded the purchase and ownership of grave plots, which could be a matter of great concern, and also recorded are the names of those who had been buried in each grave. In addition the researcher will find details of dates, addresses and relationships. Left between the pages are fragments of his correspondence with proprietors or their families which point to the care he exercised in this work, while his handwriting is a joy to read.   The weathering of many of the stones in the chapel graveyard has made them difficult to read, and the grave register can be of great help in researching names and dates. It should be remembered that the Trustees of the New Ground had decided that some plots should be made available for the burial of the poor, whose names appear in the Burial Register kept by successive ministers, but for whom no other memorial exists. The purchase by the trustees of the New Ground early in the nineteenth century had not gone smoothly, and was not finally settled until after the death of Richard Vaughan Yates. An account of the dealing is given by Laurence Hall in his history of the Ancient Chapel. Inside the chapel is a memorial tablet placed by the friends of Philip Holt.

Memorial in the Ancient Chapel to Philip Henry Holt

Charitable Work

The family of George Holt senior made a notable contribution to charitable works in the city of Liverpool. George Holt senior was aware of the views of his father, Oliver, about education, and George recognized the benefits of education, and the need for greatly improved provision for all. At the time of the Census of 1831 there were numerous schools in Liverpool, but they were of varying quality, and often required the payment of fees, which, however modest, were out of reach of the poor. The extent of literacy and illiteracy at that time cannot be decided with certainty, but efforts were being made to improve the situation. The churches, Anglican, Roman Catholic and non-conformist, conducted schools offering the beginnings of education. There were also charity schools such the School for the Blind, founded in 1791, said to be the first of its kind in the kingdom, and removed to Hardman Street in 1850, the Blue Coat School, founded in 1708 and in Moorfields a school for girls which came to the public notice in February 1810, as a result of a tragic accident when the tower of St Nicholas' Church collapsed, and a number of girls were killed. The present tower was designed by Thomas Harrison, and survived the bombing of the Second World War. There was also a grammar school, the Royal Institution School in Colquitt Street. The Liverpool Royal Institution had been founded in 1814 for "the promotion of Literature, Science and the Arts," and the trustees had gone on to found a grammar school for boys, which was very successful, but closed in 1892, at a time when the reform of schools was imminent. The Royal Institution continued in its building in Colquitt Street, its functions having been taken over by other bodies, until it was dissolved in 1948.

In 1825 a number of prominent citizens led by James Mulleneux and Richard Vaughan Yates agreed to set up by subscription the Liverpool Mechanics' School of Art. In the first years of its existence the Institution changed its name to Liverpool Mechanics' Institute and School of Arts, later to be known simply as *The Liverpool Institute*, eventually settling in its premises in Mount Street, with a foundation stone laid in 1835, and later it assumed a different role as a high school for boys. The object of the founders was to provide a school where working men could improve themselves. There is an indication here that some of the existing schools in the town had succeeded in giving their pupils a level of literacy that would enable them to undertake further study, but study after a long working day must have called for great determination. Tuition was offered in evening and day courses, there was a subscription library, while in the hall readings were given by famous writers and speakers, including Charles Dickens and Anthony Trollope. The venture succeeded in its purpose, but on the whole its clients were not well-off, and finance remained a problem. George Holt senior took a great interest, and gave considerable support, financial and practical, to the extent that he succeeded later in securing the repayment of the mortgage on the building. He was greatly concerned with the lack of schools for girls, and made available the neighbouring building, Blackburne House to be used as a grammar school for girls. After the death of George Holt senior in 1861 all of the Holt family joined in making over to the Liverpool Institute the building and grounds of Blackburne House as a memorial to their father. Over the years the members of the Holt family gave much of their time and energy in serving as directors on the management committee, and were elected to serve as president. They were also generous in their giving. William Durning Holt endowed scholarships for students to go on to university, and Alfred gave large sums to support the Institute. In 1907, following the changes in public provision brought about by the Act of 1902, the governors handed over the buildings and assets to the city council, which maintained the schools until they were closed in the 1980s following the reorganization of secondary education. The two Liverpool Institute Schools were extremely successful, with great demand for places.

George Holt junior was one of the group of citizens who worked strenuously to secure the establishment of the University College, for which he endowed two chairs. On 12th November 1904 the George Holt Physics Laboratory of the University of Liverpool was opened by Lord Kelvin.

In its obituary notice of 10th April 1896 the *Liverpool Review* commented,

> The funeral of Mr G. Holt on Wednesday afternoon was attended by a large and significant representation of the wealth, commercial enterprise, culture and philanthropy of the city. The multitude of kind deeds done by him in secret and never reported will never be known to the world.

After the death of her parents, George and Elizabeth, Emma Holt lived in their home, Sudley, in Mossley Hill. Emma bequeathed the house and its contents, including the valuable art collection of her parents, to the city of Liverpool, for the enjoyment of the people. Sudley remains a popular attraction to visitors, with the beautifully presented art collection, and a splendid view from the grounds of the River Mersey, the Wirral, and the hills beyond.

Philip Henry Holt worked all his life to secure a better life for the people. He bought a piece of land in Wavertree, had the house demolished and the site cleared and levelled, and presented it to the city as a

George Holt (1825-1896)

play area. He specified that it was his wish that it should not become a formal Victorian park, and so it has remained. There was a grand opening on 7th September 1895. Twelve thousand children were present, and in the evening a splendid display of fireworks was given. Philip had hoped to make his gift anonymously, and so the Wavertree Playgound became known to all as "The Mystery". Of course, the truth became known. For over a hundred years The Mystery has remained a playground, and has provided a welcome green space. Over the years, in order to take account of changing patterns of sport, specialist sports halls and sports grounds have been added. Philip died childless, and his will left provision for a trust fund, which has had several name-changes, and is now known as the P. H. Holt Foundation, the aim of which is to help the efforts of groups of people to set up facilities for the common good. It aims to be self-sustaining, and to manage from year to year on its income. The trustees consider applications made to them at their offices in India Buildings for grants in aid of a wide range of activities.

Sir Richard Durning Holt died during the darkest days of the war, in April 1941. His funeral service was held at Ullet Road Church, and was conducted by the Rev Lawrence Redfern. He described Sir Richard in words spoken by one of his staff:

> "He always seemed to have time for us, whether in a high or lowly place."

Further Reading

Reference was made to many books and magazines located at Liverpool Record Office including:

Transactions of the Liverpool Engineering Society

Transactions of the Unitarian Historical Society

Transactions of the Historic Society of Lancashire and Cheshire

Staff Magazine, Mersey Docks and Harbour Board

House Journals, Lamport and Holt

'Bulletin', Blue Funnel and Glen Lines

Sea Breezes

'Holt School Magazine' (December 1937)

Herbert J. Tiffen, *A History of the Liverpool Institute Schools, 1825–1935*, (Liverpool 1935).

Obituary notices in *Liverpool Daily Post, Liverpool Courier, Journal of Commerce* and *Liverpool Review*.

An Everyday History of Liverpool, two volumes, (Liverpool, Scouse Press, 1981)

NOAH JONES 1801 – 1861

Unitarian minister and founder of a Liverpool dynasty

Philip Waldron

Noah Jones was born on 13th January 1801 in Etruria, Staffordshire. Etruria was home of the Unitarian Wedgwood pottery workshops and the place of employment for Noah's father George Jones, who worked as a surveyor. Noah's mother, Sarah Jones, named her eldest son after her uncle, Reverend Noah Hill. Sarah wanted her son to be trained in the ministry and at an early age, Noah was placed under the instruction of Rev Noah Hill. In his early years he proved to have the mind and disposition for ministry; his mother's choice had been justified. Noah's parents "were anxious to teach their children the best lessons of practical religion" (Whitfield, 1861).

After performing well at school he began his ministerial training at Coward College in Wymondley, Hertfordshire. Here Noah studied to become a Congregational minister. He soon began to question the nature of orthodox doctrine. Unsatisfied by the explanations of his tutors, he was unable to conform to their expectations.

Unitarian preaching

Noah's theological stance was unsettling to many of his fellow students and tutors; his preaching contained a strong element of Socinianism. This antitrinitarian perspective caused some controversy. These "dangerous opinions" (Whitfield, 1861) would not be tolerated for long, as they were incompatible with the original constitution of the institution. At the age of nineteen, Noah Jones was asked to attend a formal meeting at the college; it was here that the tutors warned him to cease his unorthodox preaching. However, during the meeting he defended his position "firmly and modestly" (Whitfield, 1861); he agreed that he would amend his preaching if his services caused sufficient complaint, but added that "he maintained his right to examine for himself the grounds of his faith, and declared that he could only hold such a form of religion as approved itself to his own reason and conscience" (Whitfield, 1861). His tutors expressed their dislike of Unitarianism and felt that this type of thinking at their college had to be stopped. There followed several interviews with Noah Jones, during which they tried to impose the congregational creed upon him, but insisted on learning of truth through "liberal and clear conscience" (Whitfield, 1861). Not only did he stand firm, Noah was influencing other students. He was becoming a "leading spirit" within the college and his principles of a liberal faith were spreading within the institutional walls. This was "deplored and condemned" (Whitfield, 1861). During one meeting the tutors asked him for a "formal statement of his religious opinions" (Whitfield, 1861). He refused, which the tutors took offence at and considered a grievous insult. They described him as an "evil, mischievous and destroying spirit" (Whitfield, 1861) and expelled him from the college. Noah left at once, which caused an upset amongst all those students that had been touched by him; in contrast to the tutors, they described him as having "a gentle spirit and a bright and sunny disposition" (Whitfield, 1861).

Noah Jones,
from a sketch in Gateacre Chapel

The next day he arrived in London and discovered that a letter had been sent by two trustees of the college, asking that he not leave. However he was determined upon his course and had said his final farewells. He intended to complete his training in Glasgow, but before he could embark on this he received a letter from Bank Street Chapel in Bolton, inviting him to preach as a candidate, succeeding the Rev John Holland. Throughout his time at Bolton he was also asked to preach at Walmsley; this was an opportunity to network with the Bank Street Chapel congregation, where he was introduced to Emily Darbishire. The Darbishire family were active within the church and local politics. Emily's brother Charles James Darbishire was the first mayor of Bolton in 1838-39.

Noah was appointed minister at Bank Street Chapel in 1821. However it seems that there was some political tampering involved, as a letter was sent to him on behalf of the majority of the congregation; they stated that someone – presumably the Darbishires, had "unscrupulously exerted themselves in accomplishing your appointment we must say and we say it with deep regret that we have been very, very much deceived" (Green & Rawson, 1896). Noah's appointment had caused a division within the chapel as a consequence of his training in Coward College and subsequent dismissal, which caused concern amongst the congregation. During his time at Bolton he was energetic and eloquent; it was said "when I first heard him, thinking that the spirit of [Philip] Doddridge was again upon the earth" (Whitfield, 1861).

Early in his second year at Bank Street Chapel the first symptoms of consumption (Tuberculosis) became apparent and Noah was advised to end his ministry and to seek a warmer climate. He intended to go to Madeira, a Portuguese island in the Mediterranean Sea. It wasn't to be. He stayed with friends in Liverpool, who cared for him greatly, and soon recovered sufficiently to return to his congregation at Bolton. Unfortunately, in 1823 another bout of illness prevented him from performing his duties and he resigned from Bank Street Chapel.

The Liverpool spirit must have invigorated him, however, for his health and strength returned, and he was floating amongst pulpits in Paradise Street Chapel, Liverpool and Cross Street, Manchester. In 1824 he served at Paradise Street for five months, and "was presented with the thanks of the congregation for 'his very able and acceptable services'" (Roberts, 1909).

He was subsequently invited to be the minister of the newly formed congregation of Todmorden which had a working class culture. He also worked as the editor of *The Plain Speaker*, a paper focused on liberal Christianity. During this time he became ill with a malignant typhus fever and became aware of dwindling numbers in his congregation. In 1827 he decided to leave, ending his time at Todmorden.

Soon afterwards, he was invited to take charge of a small congregation in Northampton, it was in this period he was "successful in gathering together an active and united congregation. A new energy in Noah was born; he conducted three services on a Sunday and was giving lectures in the week. Also he started to become an active member in liberal politics, pushing the cause of freedom and truth" (Whitfield, 1861). He was often embroiled in debate with the local orthodox ministers; he would hold his own in arguments both verbal and written. He wouldn't be bullied into a corner with the orthodoxy of the majority, still the young student with pure ideals of searching for truth, still unbending before the tutors.

Marriage to Emily Darbishire

In 1829 he married Emily Darbishire at Manchester Cathedral, cementing the relationship which had begun at Bank Street Chapel, Bolton. Her father, Robert Darbishire, was born in Rivington and was a successful textile merchant. They were a prosperous family and there is no doubt that Emily came with a significant dowry. It is apparent that married life benefited Noah during his time at Northampton congregation and in 1830 his first child Sarah was born, presumably naming her after his mother; he held her in high regard and would often say how much he "owed to her strong yet gentle influence over him." (Whitfield, 1861) This period of his life in Northampton was seen by his friends as the best days of his ministry.

In the summer of 1832, Noah was travelling on his way to Birmingham by coach when a fellow traveller was unseated; Noah reached out to save him from falling, but lost his balance and was thrown out of the coach. He landed on a heap of stones, which was near fatal, suffering a compound fracture of the leg and a severe blow to the head. For two weeks he was in a coma, on the brink of death.

A time of convalescence took place, the care of his wife and his friends proved successful; but the shock of the accident had weakened him, and an attack of

Cholera always hung over him. After some time he returned back to his congregation, but was unable to continue the work he had so diligently begun.

In 1834 he left Northampton and took a post at Derby, Friar Gate Chapel. During the next fourteen years, he was conscious of his health and worked at a measured pace to ensure he was able to do good works for his congregation. Over this time at Derby his health improved quickly and he established a good relationship with his congregation. He discharged his pastoral duties in an exemplary manner, walking the hills from village to village to visit his parishioners. He became a member of the Temperance Society, a social movement which abstained from alcohol and petitioned the government to enact anti-alcohol legislation.

His time in Derby saw the birth of five children; in 1838 his second daughter Louisa was born, in 1840, his third daughter Frances. His first son, Charles William Jones was born in 1842 and of all these children, Charles William would prove to be the greatest success – a ship-owner, philanthropist and one of the founders of Liverpool College, now Liverpool University. In 1846 his second son Francis was born and in 1847 Arthur Edwin came into the world.

Appointment at Gateacre

In 1848 he was offered a position at Gateacre Chapel, outside Liverpool. His duties at Gateacre were light by comparison to the activities he was accustomed to. Regardless, he continued his ministry and his pastoral work. At Gateacre he suffered severe headaches and seizures, undoubtedly caused by the tragic fall that occurred in 1834. In 1849 his final child was born, Edward. Whilst at Gateacre, he introduced the first organ and this was played by his daughter Louisa. He also abolished the customary Christmas dinner at the neighbouring pub, the Bear and Staff, instead inviting the congregation to dine with him at the Manse, known as 'the Nook.'

In 1859 the headaches and seizures which had afflicted Noah for a decade stopped. In the twilight of his life, his last two years saw the "old bright and ardent spirit" (Whitfield, 1861). On Sunday, 25th August 1861, Noah had walked to the chapel and began his service as normal. He was animated and full of life during his service. The chapel was inexplicably attended by all those who were members of the chapel; it was as if there was a whispered calling for everyone to attend. Noah was unnaturally strong for all the readings, but during the final prayer, he grew noticeably weak; words began to fail him, but he was intent on continuing the service. Instead of speaking the words for the closing hymn, he pointed to the page. The congregation were so upset at seeing their minister fall into such a state they stopped the service and carried him home. Noah had suffered a stroke, disabling his speech and movement. Three days later on 28th August 1861 Noah Jones died.

He was buried at Rivington Chapel in the plot with his father and mother-in-law Robert and Sarah Darbishire. The Gateacre congregation provided for Emily to live in the Nook until she passed away on 13th January 1887 and was reunited with her beloved husband at Rivington Chapel.

As a preacher Noah Jones continued to explain and defend the "doctrines of Unitarian Christianity he was always most anxious to set forth the practical lessons of the gospel, and to speak the truth in all things boldly and fearlessly." (Whitfield, 1861) His time at Gateacre saw the ardent young student replaced by a gifted and experienced minister, comfortable with himself, his questions and his parishioners. He was a lover of the arts, music, painting and poetry. He saw the beauty in the

The grave of Noah Jones
at Rivington Chapel

everyday and would often take long walks in the surrounding area of Gateacre enjoying the natural environment. He was well-loved and affectionate friend and father whose lineage would prove to be his legacy. Much could be said of his son, Charles William Jones, the founder of Liverpool University, and his grandson Charles Sydney Jones became High Sheriff of Lancashire 1929-1930, Lord Mayor of Liverpool between 1938-42, and was knighted in 1937. In them can be seen Noah Jones and his principles of liberal Christianity.

Further Reading

Anonymous, *The Monthly Repository of Theology and General Literature,* Volume 20, (1825) (Hackney; London: Sherwood, Gilbert and Piper).

P. Green & H. Rawson, *Bank Street Chapel, Bolton. Bi-Centenary Commemoration 1696-1896,* (Hull: Elsom and Co. 1896).

B. Plent & M. Chitty, *Gateacre & Belle Vale,* (Stroud: The History Press Ltd. 2009).

H.D. Roberts, *Hope Street Church Liverpool And The Allied Nonconformity,* (Liverpool: The Liverpool Booksellers Company Ltd. 1909).

H.C. Trust, *http://todunitarianchurch.caldercats.com/njones.htm.* Retrieved August 2013, from http://todunitarianchurch.caldercats.com/. (n.d.).

E.T. Whitfield, *Unitarian Magazine and Review,* New Series, Vol XVII , (1861), 748-754.

Portrait of James Martineau by Charles Agar (1846)

JAMES MARTINEAU 1805 – 1900

Unitarian philosopher and theologian

Len W. Mooney

In Catholic France, the Edict of Nantes, 1685, caused havoc amongst Protestant Dissenters and many fled to England. One such was Gaston Martineau who settled in Spitalfields, East London. Here he married a French lady before moving to Norwich. His son Thomas became a successful woollen merchant who took as his wife a lady from Newcastle. Their son James was born in 1805. The family worshipped at the Octagon Chapel, Norwich, a Unitarian Chapel. The era was a propitious time for the birth of men who became famous; John Stuart Mill 1806: Disraeli 1804: Gladstone 1806: Tennyson 1806: John, later Cardinal, Newman 1801. Thus there were great minds James could challenge and learn from; I think he knew them all.

In the early 1800s, to preach of God as a single unit was illegal but Unitarians were quietly accepted. Although the word "Unitarian" was often used as a term of abuse; it was eventually adopted by the denomination in its title. The actual religious philosophy was still based exclusively on the acceptance of the gospels as the truth by revelation; miracles were still a main part of the belief. The 1813 Trinity Act relieved persons who impugned the doctrine of the Holy Trinity from certain penalties; this was, in effect, Unitarian Emancipation.

The general attitude towards Unitarians at that time can be judged by two observations made by William Cobbett in his book *Rural Rides*. He writes of the "Devil's Jump," three small hills at Churt in Surrey, "The Unitarians will not believe in the Trinity because they cannot account for it… will they come down to Churt and account for the placing of these three hills?" Possibly he is thinking of Calvary, certainly he knew little of geology. The second quotation is "… the Unitarians, that queer sect who will have all the wisdom of the world to themselves; who will believe and won't believe; who will be Christians and won't have a Christ; who will laugh at you if you believe in the Trinity and who would (if they could) boil you in oil if you believe in the Resurrection." He further writes that they claim, "we are the really enlightened…the exclusive patentees of *the salt of the earth* sold only at our old and original warehouse in Essex Street, in the Strand…." Essex Street is still the location of the denomination's Headquarters.

Early education

Martineau was schooled first at home, next at grammar school and finally at Lewin's Mead Meeting in Bristol, a Unitarian congregation, by the minister, Dr Carpenter. Here he became interested in the minister's philosophy of "moral feeling", the feeling that comes when the correct moral duty has been done. He left Bristol aged 16 intending to become an engineer and found a placement in Derby. Here he lodged with the Reverend Edward Higginson. While there he attended the funeral of the Reverend Henry Townsend, late minister of the Unitarian High Pavement Chapel in Nottingham. This event proved to be a turning point for him; he felt there was a purpose in his life and decided to train for the Unitarian ministry. He entered Manchester College, then at York, in 1822.

James Martineau

Higher education had been a problem for Unitarians since the Test Act, 1673, which ruled that Dissenters could not hold office unless Church of England communion had been taken, and the Act of Uniformity, 1662, which required acceptance of the 39 Articles of Faith. 2000 ministers, one third of the total ministry left the church; an event known as the Great Ejection. Another effect was basically to bar Unitarians from entering Universities. The solution to this was to start their own academies in selected towns around the country. Manchester College founded 1786 was the successor to Warrington Academy, (1756-1783). It moved to York (1803-1840) back to Manchester (1840-1853), to London (1853-1889) and finally to Oxford in 1889. In 1996 it became a full college of the University with a new name Manchester Academy and Harris College; the working name is Harris Manchester College. To further confuse matters there is the Unitarian College, Manchester, the successor to an institution founded 1854; it is affiliated to that university. Training for the ministry can take place at both places.

Martineau stayed at the college for five years studying the Bible, mathematics, philosophy, physics, Plato and Aristotle, plus a few other subjects. He took part in the usual student actives but it was obvious in the early days that he was a gifted, brilliant student of great intellect. After a year spent helping at Lewin's Mead he joined the Eustace Street congregation in Dublin as junior minister. In 1838 he became the senior and only minister which entitled him to a grant from the *Regium Donum*, a fund which dated from the time of Charles II and had been accepted by previous ministers. Because of his strong views that the church and state must be kept separate Martineau refused to accept the money; this decision split the congregation. At a congregational meeting he was defeated by the casting vote of the chairman and sacked. He paid dearly for his stance; he was without a ministry, the contact with projects he had started was ended and his house was sold at a loss.

Paradise Street

He returned to England with his family in 1839 as minister of Paradise Street chapel, Liverpool, and stayed with the congregation when it moved in 1849 to a newly built chapel in Hope Street, a short distance away. The new chapel was demolished after the war to make way for an area rebuilding scheme. Soon his brilliant oratory and theological arguments caused much concern for the Wesleyan Circuit who wanted special appointments to counter his views. The Anglican church arranged a series of sermons over thirteen weeks "to oppose the false theology of the Unitarian System". Martineau, together with other ministers held meetings the following Tuesday to argue the Unitarian case. These were attended to full capacity. He resigned from Hope Street chapel in 1851 to take up a professorship at Manchester College instructing in theology, philosophy and Hebrew. This gave him more time to develop his changing views on Unitarianism and the understanding of scripture generally.

Paradise Street Chapel

After the college moved to London in 1857 Martineau stayed in the north for two years, commuting as necessary. He became minister at Little Portland Street Chapel in central London combining this with his college work. In 1869 he was appointed Principal of Manchester College, retaining the post until resigning in 1885; he was then eighty years old. He was immediately made President of the body of Trustees, a post he held for two years.

When Martineau defended the denomination in Liverpool in the late 1830s it was still based on the total acceptance of the stories about Jesus including the miracles listed in the New Testament. It was soon after this that his views began to change. How he began to question the simple faith in the gospels is best shown by reproducing some of the arguments he used.

The path taken by his theology was influenced initially by the writings of the Reverend William E. Channing (1780-1842) who preached that, "moral perfection is the essence of God and the supreme end for man, the function of Jesus was not that of a heaven sent messenger communicating objective Faith but was to be interpreted as the manifestation of the Divine within the limits of humanity. It was the soul in Jesus which revealed the Divine character."

Divine inspiration

According to Martineau, the significance of Christianity was now raised and glorified; a fresh foundation was laid on conscience and its executive agent willpower. Once obligation became the core of moral experience the human spirit acquired a new dignity. He favoured divine inspiration and Christianity; miracles did not guarantee truth but drew attention to a person. The result is that one can be a Christian without believing in miracles. Martineau considered that Protestant Christianity begins with the influence of Paul on Martin Luther's transcendent mind, Paul claimed that Christ's wisdom came from the Law (of Moses) and the prophets and the worshipping of the God of Abraham and then back to Isaac and to Jacob and so on until we are lost in the region where the human and the divine are inextricably mixed. Thus we all live by communicated religion. He declared that the development of the church lay in Paul's plea for the gentiles to be admitted to the privilege of the gospels, circumcision was not necessary. The Greeks followed Peter's teaching and turned to Rome; others, including some Jews, followed Paul.

From his research of the gospels, Martineau claimed that the first three are anonymous documents founded no doubt on earlier material. The oldest, Matthew, did not receive its present form until AD 135; the fourth was not known until some time later. The gospels give Jesus the status of Messiah; on this Martineau wrote, "The notion of Jesus as Messiah results from the search for Christianity in the wrong place, namely, the literal creed of the first age instead of the whole generations since; 'the chief Judaic error' has been set up as 'the chief Christian verity'. The limit imposed by this faith on early Christian ethos often renders the primitive gospels inadequate for modern needs. It reasons with principles we do not own and is tinged with feelings we cannot show." This was written more than a century ago and still has much truth today

He commented on the significance which Paul gave to Jesus "Had a Messianic reign been set up in Jesus' life time, Gentiles would have been excluded. The Messiah must cease to be Jewish before he could become universal and this implied his death by which the personal relationships which made him the property of one nation could be annihilated. To this Jesus submitted".

Martineau's aim had always been to develop a religion "First Hand," straight out of the interaction between the soul and God and not to accept a "Second Hand" religion copied from anonymous traditions existing in the Eastern Mediterranean eighteen (now twenty) centuries ago.

Ethical theory

He also wrote, "if Ethics is the science of human nature two questions arise; first what is the nature of moral judgement, whence our notions of right and wrong and second what is the source of our moral ideas. Viewed from man's relation to God or nature an ethical interpretation can come from an ulterior concept which may be metaphysical. Start from an analysis of moral facts revealed by our own experience, the method becomes psychological - nothing is assumed but the existence of experience. All moral judgements are preferential and imply a choice. The choice depends on something called conscience, we choose the action with the higher moral quality". He did propose that morals should have a hierarchy, an order of rank; we should always choose the higher in the order when there were conflicting choices.

Martineau opposed any title for a religious organization which would limit its theology or any change thereof; self-sufficiency of Scripture was the right to free inquiry. Congregations founded on Open Trusts should not commit themselves to an association constituted for the promotion of a particular doctrine. This may be why the Liverpool (later Merseyside) and District Missionary Association, founded 1868, does not contain the word "Unitarian" in its title although it was and still is purely Unitarian. In his efforts to establish this view two things followed. First Martineau founded the Free Christian Union of Churches. There was some support from Unitarian Chapels but not enough to keep the Union active; it was abandoned in 1870 but the name became sufficiently important within the denomination that the words "Free Christian" are included in its formal title. The second point was, Martineau hereafter refused to enter or to preach in a chapel or church which had the word "Unitarian" in its title.

Early ecumenism

He worked out a scheme for "The National Church as a Federal Union" on the assumption that different communions divided the Truth among them and none would profess the whole of it. He wanted a church where Catholics and Unitarians - while retaining their separate forms of worship - might jointly belong. He could not believe that history could be so misread as to refuse the name Christian to any who claimed it. He failed to realize that while proposing to abolish the Act of Uniformity he was enforcing a new basic principle, namely, equal recognition of all Christian communions as members of the Universal Church. Needless to say no denomination accepted the idea, indeed they argued loudly against it, especially the Established church which would be disestablished and disendowed. Was it an early attempt at ecumenicalism?

His early writings and religious philosophy which had marked him out as an excellent intellectual was shown during his long life by the many poems, hymns and books he wrote all of which had outstanding quality and effect. He certainly became a well known figure in the western world being awarded honorary doctorate degrees by Edinburgh, Oxford and Harvard universities. If he had one drawback it was his verbosity, using ten words where three of four would have sufficed. In his 664 page book *Seat of Authority in Religion*, which had its fourth edition published in 1898, one chapter covers 99 pages, wherein his discussion of the fourth gospel, John, lasts for 47 pages. Martineau felt that John had been written by one person not by a committee of several people and was the most accurate account of the events in Jerusalem.

The interior of Hope Street Church

His view on what a sermon should be: "The preacher's function is to take out of scripture some thought so little entangled with conditions of time and place as already to speak for itself and to transfer it unchanged to the hearers' experience and duties in their different time and place". He may not have been successful himself; a member of his congregation wrote, (I paraphrase slightly) "In your preaching there is a superfluity of intellectual effort. It would be spiritually more effective if there were far less perfection of literary beauty and less condensation of refined thought and metaphor…the effort to follow your meaning is too great and impairs the pleasure and profit of listening to you".

By 1890 Martineau had retired from the ministry. In 1891 he refused an invitation to the centenary celebration of Lewin's Mead in Bristol, pleading "The time has come for me to accept the place of a quiet spectator of the scene I am about to leave". He lived for a further few years, dying on 11th January 1900.

In a speech in 1860 he spoke of "the difficulty of inducing parents to insistent obedience from the young". This situation hasn't changed much over the years but Unitarianism has. No longer is there a belief in the New Testament and its miracles; Jesus has become a great teacher not a heavenly king; conscience is the new guide based on personal religious feeling. Unitarians could think for themselves unhindered by the limits of a man made creed. The denomination may not have changed as Martineau would have wished but it was released from the stifling acceptance of Biblical texts and could move forward to a faith based on reason and an enlightened conscience. It is possible that other Christian denominations have been influenced in some degree by his works.

James and his sister Harriet, a noted author in her own right, are both buried in Highgate Cemetery, North London in an area named Dissenters' Row. The cemetery is well known as the final resting place of the good and the great; Karl Marx is interred there. Harriet receives some publicity in the guide book to the cemetery; James is mentioned solely as her brother who is buried nearby.

Further Reading

J. Estlin Carpenter, *James Martineau, Theologian and Teacher: a study of his life and thought* (London 1905).

James Drummond and C. B. Upton, *The Life and Letters of James Martineau*, 2 vols. (London 1902).

Engraving of Joseph Blanco White by F.C. Lewis

JOSEPH BLANCO WHITE 1775 – 1841

Spanish exile in Liverpool

David Steers

Among the many interesting portraits held in Ullet Road Church there is one dating from the 1820s of an Oxford don. It is a bright and attractive portrait of a man in academic bands set in a pose to emphasize his status. On his knee he holds his mortar board; to his right sits his degree certificate and the university seal; over his shoulder, beneath a plush crimson curtain, is a view of Oriel College and the University Church of St Mary the Virgin. The subject's features are sharp and attentive, his manner composed and comfortable. There could be no doubt in the mind of the viewer that this was a man at the height of his powers and well placed at the heart of Anglican Oxford.

The subject is Joseph Blanco White, fellow of Oriel College, friend of John Henry Newman, mainstay of the 'Noetic' group of Anglican clergy who attempted to provide an intellectual defence of Anglicanism on the grounds of its reasonableness. But he had travelled a long way to get to Oxford, from ultra Catholic Seville where he began his career as a devout priest and his pilgrimage was to take him further on, ultimately to end his days as a Unitarian in Liverpool, a close friend of James Martineau, John Hamilton Thom and William Rathbone.

Joseph Blanco White was born José María Blanco y Crespo on 11th July 1775 in Seville, into a devoutly Catholic family, the son of a merchant and his wife. His own name reflects his mixed Spanish and Irish heritage. His mother, María Gertrudis Crespo y Neve, was a member of a Spanish noble family, his father, Guillermo Blanco y Morrogh, was the son of William White who had emigrated from

Joseph Blanco White, portrait in Ullet Road Church

69

Waterford earlier in the century to establish an import-export business.

Destined for a job in the family firm Blanco White discovered a vocation for the priesthood. Naturally pious as a youth his devotion soon was outstripped by an intellectual curiosity that set him at odds with the prevailing religious climate. Seville was characterized by an intensity of religious devotion. In his autobiography he recalled the onerous discipline of the religious life of the university, regarding much of it as a "mischevious absurdity". Later, as a young priest, he remembered his distaste for an occasion on which he had to preach to a congregation in a darkened crypt who were forced to lash themselves with knotted scourges after the service. He remembered throughout his life being taken as a boy of eight to see the burning of the body of a woman who had been garrotted for heresy.

He commenced his studies at the University of Seville in 1790 but found little inspiration in the traditional course on offer and allowed his intellect to range more widely, not least through membership with like-minded friends of a private Academy of Belles-Lettres. But Blanco White remained loyal to his church, with perhaps a leaning towards Jansenist, reforming tendencies. He did well academically, was ordained a priest in 1799 and soon after was rewarded with a royal chaplaincy at the Chapel of St Ferdinand in Seville and an appointment as Rector of the Collegio Mayor. As a member of the higher clergy he was excused any pastoral or parochial responsibilities, his career was set fair for comfortable and successful progress. But he found himself increasingly beset by doubts about the Church in which he had been ordained and at odds with the authorities over the limits they placed on learning and the free spread of knowledge.

Leaves the priesthood

In 1805 he gained leave to move to Madrid where he left the priesthood, fathered a child and immersed himself in literary and political matters. He knew he could no longer continue as a priest, to do so, he wrote, would be to be an impostor and a hypocrite, but to resign would bring punishment and disgrace on himself and his family. In 1808 his problems were brought to head by the French invasion of Spain under Napoleon. He threw himself in with the nationalist movement resisting the invaders, penning pamphlets and anti-French tracts. But the success of the French invasion made continued resistance fruitless and, disguised as an Englishman, Blanco White escaped from Spain in 1810, aware that he would never see his homeland again.

He made his way to London where he was sheltered by Lord Holland and his friends, including the auctioneer James Christie. In exile he continued to contribute to the Spanish resistance, becoming editor of *El Español*, a nationalist journal. He renounced the Catholic Church and joined the Church of England, becoming accepted as an Anglican priest in 1814.

A combination of evangelical theology, anti-Catholic zeal and his skill and capability as a writer brought him to the attention of the dominant faction within Anglicanism and also to the authorities who from 1812 paid him an annual pension from government funds of £250. His writings in the cause of the Spanish resistance were instrumental in this but the increasing radicalism of his thought including calls for constitutional reform and for the granting of self-government to the Spanish-American dominions marked him out as a traitor in the eyes of the Spanish government. A few years later his status as a man of letters in the English language was secured by the contribution of his 'Letters from Spain' to the *New Monthly Magazine* under the pseudonym Don Leucadio Doblado, a pun in Spanish of the name Blanco White.

Fellowship at Oriel College

His reception into his adopted country was confirmed by the granting of a fellowship at Oriel College, at the time the most brilliant of all the Oxford Colleges in 1826. This followed the publication of *Practical and Internal Evidence Against Catholicism*, a pamphlet opposing the granting of toleration to Roman Catholics.

At Oriel he became particularly friendly with a young Fellow of the College – John Henry Newman, at that time holding similar evangelical views as him but someone whose own pilgrimage would take him in an opposite direction towards Rome and a Cardinal's hat. Together they played violin duets in the College.

It was at this point in his career that the portrait that now hangs in Ullet Road was painted. But if that portrait represents the high point of achievement for a man exiled from his native country and prospering at the intellectual and spiritual heart of a new one it also conceals the growing doubts and uncertainties he was grappling with.

His opposition to the Catholic Church would never waver but for a democrat like him he came to question the fittingness of excluding Catholics from national life. He renounced his previous views – which he now described as being born under "the Spirit of the Episcopal Popery of England" - and came to support the emancipation of Catholics, which caused him to be attacked and abused in Oxford.

Not only that, for a long time he had struggled with many Anglican doctrinal beliefs, not least with the doctrine of the Trinity. With this came a belief in the unsuitability of established churches and a rejection of the need to subscribe to prescribed creeds.

His time in Oxford proved not to be especially creative and the growing gulf that now developed between his position and its intellectual and theological underpinning meant that moving on was inevitable. Ironically, despite his remarks about "the Episcopal Popery of England," it was to a bishop's palace that he moved.

Richard Whately had been a fellow of Oriel and a colleague and friend. When he was unexpectedly offered the position of Archbishop of Dublin Blanco White followed him to live in his home and act as tutor to his son in 1832. Whately represented a more liberal strand within Anglican thought but Blanco felt increasingly uncomfortable publishing works that questioned Anglican doctrines from an Archbishop's home. He had, in any case, reached a view that all established churches were the enemies of freedom of thought and liberty of conscience.

Moves to Liverpool

In January 1835 Blanco White moved to Liverpool and found himself, for the first time, amongst Unitarians. Here he found a spiritual home unlike anything he had previously known. He was exiled from his native Spain, suffered bouts of ill-health and detested the English climate, but felt at one with the Unitarians in Liverpool. This was forged from a very deep sense of sympathy. His closest friends were ministers like James Martineau and particularly John Hamilton Thom to whom he wrote on 31st July 1836 after attending morning service at Renshaw Street Chapel:

> I am become so incorporated and associated with your congregation that, though unacquainted with most of those who compose it, I always return with that feeling of satisfaction which arises from having met one's friends. It does me good to see the faces with which I am now familiar; and I bring back a secret assurance that I have been in company with a considerable number of kind-hearted, benevolent, and upright people, who have a certain sympathy with me, and would be glad to show it me if an opportunity offered…the members of a congregation should know each other, at least, by sight; there should exist a degree of fraternity among them. Would heaven that manners and national temper admitted of making the religious meetings of Unitarians still more social! But I must not indulge my *radicalism*; there is enough, and more than enough, to make me every day rejoice in the company the particular class of Christians with whom I am associated.

But it was not just a close sense of fellow-feeling with the Unitarian congregations, there was also a deeper sense of intellectual convergence. Writing in the previous year (8th February 1835) to the Rev George Armstrong after listening to James Martineau preach in Paradise Street Chapel he expressed this:

> What a relief it was to me, to be able to join in social worship, undisturbed by offensive expressions, and without the necessity of mental protests and reservations at every step! The humblest hearer might join "not only with his voice, but with his understanding," in praising God, and praying for blessings spiritual and temporal.

He soon became absorbed into the Unitarian community in Liverpool and was one of the early supporters of the Liverpool Domestic Mission, proposing at the foundation meeting of April 1836 that:

> The appropriate duties of the Minister for the Poor shall be, to establish an intercourse with a limited number of families of the neglected poor, to put himself into close sympathy with their wants and feelings, to become to them a Christian adviser and friend, to promote the order and comfort of their homes, and the elevation of their social tastes, to bring them into a permanent connexion with religious influences, and, above all, to promote an effective education to their children, and to shelter them from corrupting agencies.

He died at Greenbank, the home of William Rathbone, on 20th May 1841 and was buried in the graveyard of Renshaw Street Chapel.

Legacy

Before his death Blanco had made his friend John Hamilton Thom his literary executor and he published his autobiography and correspondence in three volumes in 1845. The publication was attended by much controversy, many of Blanco's former Anglican friends, including Richard Whately, disassociated themselves from it very strongly, and reviewers such as W.E. Gladstone were horrified by it. Curiously Thom's *Life* of Blanco White was also instrumental in directing J.H. Newman towards Rome, finally convincing him that there could be no happy medium between 'Pantheism' and the claims of Rome.

But although his immediate legacy was fraught with controversy and although his theological thought and writings were perhaps of most importance to him all this soon died away and it took a long time for

Memorials to Blanco White in Mount Pleasant

Blanco's literary reputation to be restored. In Spain, as the 20th century progressed, there was a gradual growth in appreciation of his poetry and writings, in his place as a recorder of Spanish life and advocate of reform which has gradually restored his reputation. In 1984 representatives of local government in Seville and the University of Seville came to Liverpool to unveil a plaque in his memory which is fixed to the memorial in Mount Pleasant which stands in the former graveyard of Renshaw Street Chapel. The Spanish delegation were joined by local political and academic representatives and the Rev Graham Murphy minister at Ullet Road Church at the time who also took part in the ceremony.

It was fitting that tribute should be paid to a Spanish exile who had made his home in Liverpool, one whose quest for truth had led him to explore many expressions of religious life, but who did not rest until he came to this city. Above all he displayed an integrity in his life that resulted in exile, illness, antagonism and hatred at different times. He could have stayed in Spain and perhaps become a bishop, he certainly could have remained a Fellow of his Oxford College or he could have lived in comfort in an Archbishop's palace in Dublin. However he took none of these routes because he chose instead to follow the dictates of his own conscience.

Further Reading

John Hamilton Thom, (ed.), *The life of the Rev. Joseph Blanco White*, 3 vols. (London 1845)

Martin Murphy, *Blanco White: self-banished Spaniard* (New Haven, London 1989)

Tony Cross, *Joseph Blanco White. Don José Maria Blanco y Crespo. Stranger and Pilgrim* (Liverpool 1984)

KITTY WILKINSON 1786 – 1860

Founder of the first public wash-house in Liverpool

Daphne Roberts

Kitty Wilkinson was born Catherine Seaward (or Seward), in county Londonderry, Ireland. Following the death of her father while she was still a child the family moved to Liverpool in 1794, but unfortunately her baby sister was drowned during a violent storm. This affected her mother very deeply and she never really got over the blow, as a consequence Kitty had to look after her for many years up to her death.

On first arrival in Liverpool she and her mother, who could read and write and was a skilled spinner and lace maker, found a home with a Mrs Lightbody, a kindly lady and a Unitarian, who employed Mrs Seaward to pass on her skills to her other servants. It was she who by her charitable example influenced Kitty in later life. However after her mother had a breakdown and was unable to work, Kitty, at the age of only 11 or 12, became an apprentice at the Caton cotton mill near Lancaster. Life must have been hard but she always retained fond memories of her time there remembering in later life: "If ever there was a heaven upon earth, it was that apprentice-house, where we were brought up in such ignorance of evil, and where Mr Hudson, the manager was a father to us all."

Kitty Wilkinson

On her return to Liverpool in around 1804 both her and her mother worked as domestic servants, but five years later Kitty set up school to teach children to read, write and sew, gathering together ninety-three pupils who were taught in one room. Her mother's lace was also sold to support them both. But unfortunately after her mother again became ill she had to close the school.

Kitty's first marriage was to Jean de Monte, a French sailor. This was a happy marriage, but sadly in 1812 her husband drowned and Kitty was left to support her two children and her increasingly frail mother. As a result she had to take work in the fields and as a charwoman before finding employment in a nail factory, and subsequently in domestic service. Her final employer was a widowed church worker, and when he died he left her a mangle; this proved to be a turning point in her life. She began to take in washing.

In 1823 she married Tom Wilkinson whom she had originally met as an apprentice in Caton cotton mill. At this time Liverpool was changing as the richer people moved to the outskirts of the city and living conditions deteriorated for the poorer classes in the overcrowded slum areas. In 1832 a cholera epidemic swept through the city due to lack of clean water and no facilities for washing. Tom and Kitty allowed all the families in their street to use their hot water boiler to wash and disinfect bedding and clothes. In this they were supported by the Liverpool District Provident Society and the Rathbone family. Those who could contributed a penny towards the costs. Kitty also assisted the doctors by helping to administer the prescribed remedies and reporting back to them the progress made, and making porridge everyday for sixty people. Alongside this she displayed many acts of kindness towards widows and orphans in the district.

First public wash-house

Because she understood the need for cleanliness she fought for the provision of public baths and wash-houses, but it was not until 1842 that the first publicly funded wash-house was built in Upper Frederick Street, the first in the country, with Tom and Kitty appointed as superintendents, Tom to manage the machinery and Kitty to supervise the washing.

In 1846 Kitty was honoured at Carnatic Hall and presented with a silver tea service by the Mayoress, Mrs George Lawrence. Inscribed on the teapot was 'The Queen, the Queen Dowager, and the Ladies of Liverpool to Catherine Wilkinson, 1846'. Soon after this Thomas Wilkinson died. Whilst supporting Kitty in her work, he had also done much for others, and a sermon given at his death by the Rev John Hamilton Thom the minister of Renshaw Street Chapel, where he had worshipped said that he was "little known by those around him, and not seeking to be known, and not knowing his own worth, yet a hero".

For a further four years Kitty and one of her sons continued to run the washhouse, but when it was demolished and replaced they lost their jobs. Fortunately ladies of Liverpool society recognizing Kitty's exceptional merit collected enough money to purchase a small annuity for her. She died in 1860 at the age of 73. In her later years she also had attended Renshaw Street Chapel and it was here that the Rev John Hamilton Thom preached her funeral service. She was buried in St James's Cemetery, where her memorial stone still survives. But her memory also lives on in a stained glass window in the Lady Chapel of Liverpool Cathedral.

Further Reading

Elizabeth Ashworth, *Champion Lancastrians* (Wilmslow c.2006)

Robert Spears, *Memorable Unitarians*, (London 1906).

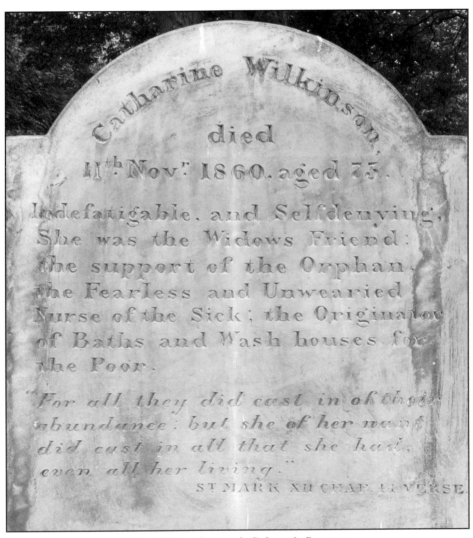

Kitty Wilkinson's grave in St James's Cemetery.
Her full name was generally spelt Catherine during her life time.

The Good Samaritan window Gateacre Chapel, presented by Sir Henry Tate

JOHN JOHNS 1801 – 1847

First Missioner to the Poor at the Liverpool Domestic Mission

David Steers

One of the great Unitarian contributions to social progress in Britain in the nineteenth century was the Domestic Mission movement. The Domestic Mission in Liverpool was not quite the first to be founded but it was the longest lasting and throughout all of its existence was a creative and innovative agency in south Liverpool. The idea for the Liverpool Domestic Mission grew out of a sermon preached in Renshaw Street Chapel by the Rev John Hamilton Thom on Christmas Day 1835. Thom and his fellow Unitarians recognized the need for a special mission to the growing numbers of poor who lived in squalor in the city's docklands. The traditional notion of a missionary is of someone who goes out into a particular field with a view to converting people to whatever beliefs the missionary might hold. This was not intended to be the model for Unitarian missionaries to the poor. The appointment of the Rev John Johns as the first minister to the poor in the winter of 1836 was to make it one of the major agencies for assisting the poor in Toxteth in the mid-nineteenth century.

A medium of kind and Christian connection

John Hamilton Thom took his cue from Joseph Tuckerman who had founded a ministry at large in Boston in 1826. He had corresponded with leading Unitarians in Britain and advanced a view of missionary work to the poor which fitted in well with the world view of patrician, manufacturing and ship-owning Unitarians in Liverpool. Writing to Sir John Bowring in 1831 Tuckerman had declared that he did not just hope for the gospel to be preached to the poor but that "a Christian sense of their relations and duties to the poor and ignorant should be understood and felt by the cultivated and by the rich". So the rich should feel a sense of community with the poor and the missionaries should provide a connection between them; "I would that a class of men should arise who will stand between the extremes of society, as a medium of kind and Christian connection between them."

In his Christmas Day sermon of 1835 Thom had described the kind of person necessary for this work; "He must be no hewer of wood or drawer of water, who is to inspire the very poorest with worthy views of their nature and their destiny… He must be no ordinary man, and have no ordinary knowledge of human nature… The ministry from which alone we venture to expect great good must be that of a man who will consecrate to it his life and his mind, who takes it as his mission on earth, who knows…no other interest, so dear to him; who lives in it and for it, who thinks on it by night and by day and whose education and menial training have qualified him to act upon human nature"

The person selected to fill this role was John Johns. Unlike most of the domestic missioners appointed by Unitarians at this time Johns was well-educated and came from within the English Presbyterian tradition rather than the working class and more emphatically Unitarian movements that were then flourishing in the north and midlands. John Johns was born in Plymouth in 1801 and educated at Plymouth Grammar School and Edinburgh University. From 1821 he was minister of the Unitarian Chapel in Crediton in Devon where he seems to have pursued a quiet country ministry keeping up wide literary interests and writing a good deal of poetry, much of which was published by the *Monthly Repository*. He also

John Johns, from a drawing in Ullet Road Church

wrote a number of hymns the best known of which is "Come Kingdom of our God", which became very popular amongst Unitarians and featured in many non-conformist hymnbooks, most recently in *Hymns of Faith and Freedom*.

It may seem surprising then that the committee of the Liverpool Domestic Mission should call Johns (on the recommendation of James Martineau). Described as "a remarkable looking man, very thin with a very benevolent countenance", he was remembered by Thom in later years as a man who looked "as sensitive as if he had no skin." Yet it proved to be an inspired choice because Johns was, as Thom later recollected, "the practical mystic, with whom the trust in God, which we all profess, is simply so absolute that it is but a natural consequence that it should become the passion for his being to turn the visions of faith into the realities of life."

Ministry begins

On being called to Liverpool to take up his new post Johns was horrified by the poverty of the people of his district. The area for the mission had been designated as the region between Greenland Street and Norfolk Street where most people lived in appalling insanitary conditions. Johns himself described the district as:

> Streets, for the most part, dark and narrow, dirty and ill-paved; houses, which are very often in the worst possible repair; rooms in lodging-houses, which are deficient in every important requisite conducive to health, convenience, and decency and cellars which....are ...damp, dark, and ruinous, and more like graves dug for the living than their homes.

Johns threw all his energy into assisting the people of his district and like other missions in Toxteth was involved in the distribution of charity. In the beginning this took the form of monetary grants but as time went on was accompanied by relief in the form of food or clothing so that by 1840 over 1,400 cases of food relief alone were being given in a year. However, Johns recognized that administering relief could never be enough in itself and that the poor should be encouraged to help themselves. In addition Johns also came to realize that an attack on the causes of poverty would be the only effective way to success. Writing in his first report Johns revealed an awareness of his own guilt:

> The Physical state of my people has been such as to touch my heart with honest shame and sorrow. As an individual of those classes, whose long alienation from them has tended to reduce them to circumstances of such unspeakable distress, I have at times felt a strong feeling of guiltiness come over me.

A central part of his work was to encourage the spread of education among the local children and he campaigned for the setting up of local free schools, himself establishing a ragged school which also served the purpose of helping to reduce the practice of street selling by children. Such ventures created a need for premises and in 1838 the first Mission House was opened in Greenland Street. Here Johns was able to set up a Mechanics Institute and a free library as well as hold religious services, but he continued with his regular visits of the district providing charity, encouraging saving and establishing a Friendly Loan Society.

A major problem was always drunkenness which Johns tried to combat by calling for an end to the practice of paying dock labourers on a Saturday evening. Johns was also a major figure in the campaign for improvements in the living and working conditions of the poor. He argued for shorter working hours and also called for more open spaces for the poor, acquiring sixteen acres of land from Lord Sefton's agent which he divided up into 143 plots and let out as allotments to the poor. His criticisms of the bad building practices that produced dwellings without proper light, ventilation and water caused the Council to take a closer interest in drainage and street cleaning and as a result typhoid became less prevalent.

Irish famine

By the mid-1840s Johns had made some progress but this was soon to be halted. The Irish famine brought thousands of destitute immigrants to Liverpool which increased the demand for charity and again increased the incidence of disease. Johns continued his work until 1847 when he contracted typhoid while attending to a sufferer who, apart from a Catholic priest who also died, no one else would touch. Although Johns's own work was to end here many of his ideas about social reform were later to provide the basis for action by the state. After two years working among the poor Johns had observed "that do what you will with humanity, you cannot wholly quench the divine ray within it."

The epitaph on his memorial stone in the Mission Chapel described him in the following terms:

Sacred to the Memory of The Rev John Johns first Minister to the Poor of the Liverpool Domestic Mission Society.

Born a Poet, and having his natural delight in a Poet's contemplation of the Works of God, he left the retired Ministry that seemed most congenial to him, amid the calm beauty of his native Devon, and became the Friend and daily Companion of the poor in crowded, woe-worn streets, there to draw forth the holier beauty of man's spiritual nature in conditions of severest trial and to find for himself a more real Communion with God in the faith, patience and penitence of the most afflicted of His children. He lived in the spirit of his great office and died its sacrifice. In a time of Pestilence the Death Angel met him across the bodies of the stricken, whom be was tending with his own hands.

Born at Plymouth, March 17, 1801. Appointed Minister to the Congregation of English Presbyterians, Crediton, Devon, January 21, 1821. Became First Minister to the Poor, Liverpool, December 16, 1836. Died June 23, 1847.

Further Reading

Anne Holt, *A ministry to the poor: being the history of the Liverpool Domestic Mission Society, 1836-1936* (Liverpool, 1936)

Anne Holt, 'John Johns: Liverpool's first minister to the poor' *Transactions of the Unitarian Historical Society (TUHS)* 6:1 (1935) 44-50

Brian A. Packer, 'The founding of the Liverpool Domestic Mission and its development under the ministry of John Johns' *TUHS* 18:2 (1984) 39-53

David Steers, 'The origin and development of the Domestic Mission movement in Liverpool and Manchester' *TUHS* 21:2 (1996) 79-103

R.J. Ash, *Christianity, community and social concern: a history of the Liverpool Domestic Mission Society from 1836*, (Liverpool 2011)

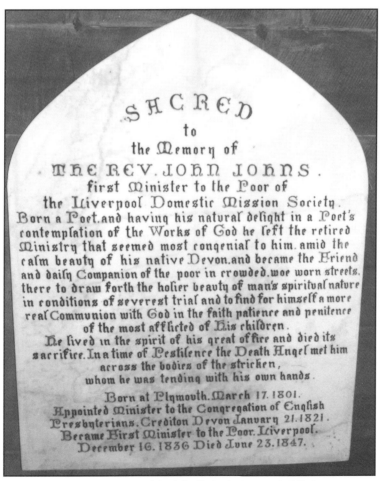

John Johns's memorial originally in the Domestic Mission
now in Ullet Road Church

St Matthew's Church, formerly Key Street Meeting House, the precursor of Paradise Street Chapel.
Lithograph by W.G. Herdman 1843.

WILLIAM HENRY CHANNING 1810 – 1884

American preacher in Liverpool

Richard Merritt

William Henry Channing was a nineteenth century Unitarian clergyman, writer and philosopher, a strong adherent of transcendentalism and one of the early supporters of the socialist movement.

Born in Boston in 1810, and brought up by his uncle, William Ellery Channing (one of the leading Unitarian thinkers of the early nineteenth century), William Henry graduated from Harvard and following ordination as a Unitarian minister took up several pastoral appointments and supported transcendental and socialist projects (for example the Brook Farm project which promised its participants a portion of the profits from the farm in exchange for performing an equal share of the work).

In 1853 he became the minister of the Unitarian church in Rochester, New York where he also became active in abolitionism. His radicalism made it difficult for him to secure pulpits in America, and this helped influence his decision to go to England in 1854.

William Henry Channing

Arrival in Liverpool

For three years he served at the Renshaw Street Chapel in Liverpool, and then assumed James Martineau's old pulpit at Hope Street Chapel, also in Liverpool.

According to Thomas Wentworth Higginson (*Heralds of a Liberal Faith* Vol III)

> there was no more distinguished position in the liberal pulpit than this [Hope Street Chapel], and he held his own in it. His thrilling eloquence reached, to an extent that surprised his friends, the English mind, which

is commonly held to be conservative. He was profoundly interested in English public affairs - what question was there, indeed, which did not interest him profoundly? - and especially in all that related to social progress and the condition of the poor.

Channing spent most of the remaining years of his life in England, which his wife and children enjoyed as their true home. He returned to America during the Civil War to serve as Chaplain to the US House of Representatives, and also minister to the Unitarian society in Washington, DC frequently helping with the war effort by visiting the battlefields and the hospitals, giving his time to the work of the Sanitary Commission and the Freedman's Bureau, and doing valiant service in the cause of the union and for emancipation. He returned to England at the close of the war, preaching in London and elsewhere.

Throughout his life Channing was a great thinker and writer. He published biographies of William Ellery Channing and Margaret Fuller Ossoli, but he also contributed to many publications and among his inspirational writings his "Symphony", is particularly famous:

> To live content with small means; to seek elegance rather than luxury, and refinement rather than fashion; to be worthy, not respectable, and wealthy, not rich; to listen to stars and birds, babes and sages, with open heart; to study hard; to think quietly, act frankly, talk gently, await occasions, hurry never; in a word, to let the spiritual, unbidden and unconscious, grow up through the common -- this is my symphony.

Transcendentalist

Channing was a member of the Transcendentalists Club. Among transcendentalists' core beliefs was an ideal spiritual state that 'transcends' the physical and empirical and is only realized through the individual's intuition, rather than through the doctrines of established religions. Channing corresponded with Ralph Waldo Emerson (and baptized his children) but did not always agree fully with Emerson's views. In particular he tended more towards a socialist approach, opining that

> the race is inspired as well as the individual; that humanity is a growth from the Divine Life as well as man; and indeed that the true advancement of the individual is dependent upon the advancement of a generation, and that the law of this is providential, the direct act of the Being of beings.

Renshaw Street Chapel

This was the ground of his Christian faith and of his reconciliation with the church. "The race is to me," he said, "a revelation of God more than any one man is, more than all separate men are." He believed that the highest products of human achievement, such as language, law, civilization, religion, and ethical development, are the results of social growth, and not of individual attainment.

"A most delightful man," wrote Theodore Parker of him, "full of the right spirit...of the most remarkable beauty of character; full of good tendencies, of noblest aspirations; an eye to see the evils of society, a heart to feel them, a soul to hope better things; a willingness to endure all self-denial to accomplish the end whereto he is sent."

He died on 23rd December 1884 in London where after his period of ministry in Liverpool he had spent the larger part of his life.

Further Reading

Anne Holt, *Walking Together: A Study in Liverpool Non-conformity 1688-1938* (London 1938)

Samuel A. Eliot (ed.), *Heralds of a Liberal Faith*, 4 vols. (Boston 1901 & 1952)

Benn's Garden Chapel. Lithograph by W.G. Herdman 1843.

CHARLES PIERRE MELLY 1829 – 1888

Creator of free water fountains and the Liverpool Olympic Festival

John Keggen

In the cloisters of Ullet Road Church there is a memorial plaque somewhat smaller than most of the other memorials to the great Unitarian worthies of the past. The smallness of the plaque rather belies the significance of the man and his contribution to the welfare of the citizens of Liverpool. It is dedicated to the memory of Charles Pierre Melly born 25th May 1829, died 10th November 1888.

Below the name and dates is the inscription "Whom The Lord Loveth He Chasteneth" The quotation is taken from Revelation chapter 3 verse 19.

This verse of scripture is not a usual one to be found as an epitaph. The word 'chasteneth' means 'punishment'. One dictionary definition reads; "to free from faults by punishing." I can only think that his relatives and friends, on witnessing the distress that Charles Melly experienced through his lifetime as a sufferer of extreme bouts of depression, culminating with him taking his own life with his own pistol, had behind it some meaning known to God. In the 21st century we might have a different viewpoint on the issue of mental illness.

One of his descendants, the jazz singer George Melly, is quoted as saying of him "He was a melancholy philanthropist who committed suicide." Charles Melly was much more than this. He was a man of great vision with ideas of an innovative, practical nature and he had the capacity to carry them out to the benefit of his fellow citizens for his own and future generations. The fact that he achieved so much whilst also suffering from a debilitating mental illness speaks volumes for his innate courage and perseverance in making the lot of his fellowmen a much easier and happy one.

Influence of Geneva

His father André Melly hailed from Geneva. He married Maria Greg the youngest daughter of the cotton mill owner and Unitarian Samuel Greg. Samuel Greg was much enlightened for his time especially in regard to the kind and humane treatment he gave to his mill workers at Quarry Bank Mill, near Wilmslow. This was very much in contrast to the practice in other mills and factories at the time. Having Maria for his mother who had imbibed from her childhood the Greg's Unitarian principles of kindness to their workers and the need for better educational opportunities for all children must have had a profound effect on Charles as he grew up. He was born in Tuebrook then a rural outlying district of Liverpool.

Charles himself was to marry Louise Forget of Geneva, his father's home town, and they had eight children.

Charles settled in Liverpool, the city of his birth and the main port for the cotton trade, which business he entered. His outlook was always a cosmopolitan one partly through his wife's and his own family's connections with Geneva. He paid many visits to Geneva and other parts of the Continent. He naturally would compare Geneva with Liverpool. He observed in Geneva the many drinking fountains placed round and about the city, items which were absent in Liverpool. In Geneva water was the property of the town authorities but it was supplied free of cost to the people, who could collect it from the fountains or pay someone to collect it. Liverpool, in a way, might have been thought to be in

Charles and Louise Melly

advance of Geneva in that water was piped into many houses, but there was a water rate to be paid. There was no provision of free drinking fountains in the streets. Charles in the course of his business visited the docks and observed that the workers couldn't relieve their thirst except by going into the ale houses and there paying for a stronger and perhaps less refreshing drink, no doubt some of them becoming more intoxicated than refreshed as the day wore on. At that time in the 1850s many people in Liverpool were emigrants in transit from Ireland and the Continent on their way to America, Australia and other places. There was no provision of drinking water for them. Being in transit they were often in distress through the lack of water, both they - and workers and dockers - were at times glad enough to drink from the horse troughs at the docks.

Charles had the first granite fountain erected at the south end of Princes Dock in March 1854. Three months later in a 12 hour period it was observed that no less than 2,336 people used the fountain. Other Melly Fountains were to be placed around the city streets. From his own purse he donated £500 towards the cost, quite a fortune in those days. He also provided wayside benches for weary walkers to take rest. Another of the benefits he achieved for the people of Liverpool came when he was Chairman of the Parks Committee. He negotiated the acquisition of the land now known as Sefton Park, still such a much valued 'green lung' and recreational space in the city. One can only speculate that had this not been done at the time it might have become subject to urban sprawl, instead of the stately park enjoyed by so many people today.

The Liverpool Olympics

The modern Olympics began in Athens in 1896 but 34 years prior to this, in 1862, Charles Melly and his friend John Hulley, a physical fitness expert, instituted the Liverpool Olympic Festival. This took place on the Mount Vernon Parade Ground on 14th June. Crowds of between 7,000 and 10,000 gathered for the event which included running, walking, high jump, long jump, pole leap, boxing, wrestling, and gymnastics. Altogether five gold, 22 silver and 23 bronze medals were awarded. The next year the 'Liverpool Olympics' attracted 15,000 spectators and competitors from much farther afield. In the following year the games were moved to the Zoological Gardens on West Derby Road, but by then some nefarious commercial activities were taking place alongside them so the fourth games were moved Llandudno. The games were held in Llandudno for a second time in 1866 but were to return to Liverpool and be held for the last time in 1867. Financial problems were thought to be the reason for the Liverpool Games coming to an end, but the idea, which had started the modern Olympics, had been sown.

Charles Melly and John Hulley were to open the Liverpool Gymnasium on Myrtle Street, and with representatives from London and Berlin the National Olympian Association was founded with the motto *Civium Vires Civitatis Vis* (the power of the state lies with the strength of its citizens).

Charles with his thoughts on universal education founded the first night school in Liverpool at Beaufort Street in 1852. One of his interests being in the Working Men's Improvement Society. He also helped to found the North End Domestic Mission in Liverpool, based on Joseph Tuckerman's Unitarian mission

Charles Melly's memorial in the cloisters, Ullet Road Church

work in Boston, Massachusetts. Liverpool, like Boston, had a rapidly expanding population and Unitarian Missions were set up to give both spiritual and practical sustenance and guidance to the many inhabitants of the city who, by dint of over-crowding and poverty, needed to be befriended and helped. He was also involved in the 'ragged schools', an extension of the Sunday School movement.

Charles Melly will perhaps be best known for the Melly Fountains, but he should be remembered for so much more. He was in the style of many Victorian philanthropists who felt that the benefits of physical education, fresh water and a decent diet should be enjoyed by all classes. His Unitarian faith was without doubt a driving power in his endeavours. It is hard to believe that a man who achieved so much in his life was at the same time afflicted with severe bouts of depression. We have even more reason to give thanks for him for the fortitude he displayed in giving so much to the benefit of his fellow citizens.

Further Reading

David Charters 'How we lit the Olympic Flame' *Daily Post*, 8th August 2008.

Patrick Neill 'Charles Pierre Melly and his Drinking Fountains', http://www.liverpoolmonuments.co.uk/drinking/mellycharles02.html

SIR HENRY TATE 1819 – 1899

Sugar refiner and major benefactor to the arts

Richard Merritt

Sir Henry Tate's beginnings were relatively humble and his formal education finished when he was barely in his teens but he was, however, to become one of the country's most successful businessmen and most generous benefactors.

Sir Henry Tate, portrait in Ullet Road

Henry was born on 11th March 1819, son of Rev William and Agnes Tate. William was a Unitarian minister in Chorley Lancashire from 1799 to 1836. With a large family to support (Henry was the eleventh son!) as a second source of income William set up a private school for poor children where Henry was educated. In addition to this - his only formal education – it became clear that Henry had learned much from his father's example in terms of hard work and "good works".

Sugar refiner

In 1832, at the age of thirteen, he became an apprentice in his brother's grocery shop in Liverpool and by the age of 20 he had bought his own shop in Old Haymarket, expanding this by 1857 to six retail outlets with additionally a wholesale business. From 1859 he was also running a cane sugar refinery in Manesty Lane, Liverpool with business partner, John Wright. Within ten years Henry Tate had disposed of his shops and, with Wright's withdrawal, was the sole owner of two refineries under the name Henry Tate & Sons.

Faced with serious competition from subsidised beet sugar imports, Tate responded by exploiting ever more sophisticated manufacturing techniques. In 1870 a new, up-to-date refinery was built in the Vauxhall area of Liverpool, in

Love Lane. Then from 1878 a factory built in London took innovation even further, in particular exploiting Tate's purchase of the sole British rights for the effective and profitable mass production of cubed sugar. Up to that time sugar had been sold in block form, to be broken up before use. Soon *Tate's Cubed Sugar* became famous throughout the world. Henry Tate retired in 1896, his son William Henry taking over the company which eventually amalgamated to become Tate and Lyle. Liverpool's Tate and Lyle factory in Love Lane continued production until 1981 when it was still producing 300,000 tons per year. Closure was blamed on a surplus of sugar as a result of the European Community's Common Agricultural Policy.

Generous donor

Although in 1881 Sir Henry moved to live at Park Hill near Streatham Common, his connections with Liverpool were considerable. As described above, sugar was produced at the Liverpool site he established for over a hundred years. It was also his home for much of his life. He lived with his first wife in the city and his children were born there. He was a Liverpool JP and briefly served on Liverpool Council. He gave £20,000 to Liverpool's Hahnemann Hospital (a homeopathic institution) and £8,000 to Liverpool Infirmary. He supported many Unitarian causes in the city including the Liverpool North End Domestic Mission and Gateacre Chapel to whom he presented a beautiful stained glass window depicting Jesus's parable of the Good Samaritan. He was also a joint benefactor (with Sir John Brunner, the chemical industrialist and liberal MP) of Ullet Road Church's cloister and the attractive (now Grade 1-listed) church hall.

Apart from his considerable role in providing employment to many thousands of workers over the years perhaps his greatest contribution to Liverpool was as one of the main benefactors of Liverpool College, later to become the University of Liverpool. He supported the initial setting up of its foundation, together with its library, research scholarships and various other donations altogether said to total £42,500, a huge sum in those times.

Tate Gallery

Of course the most famous example of Henry Tate's philanthropy is his establishment of London's *National Gallery of British Art*, more commonly known as the "Tate Gallery". The story of how this was established warrants a book in itself. Since moving to his house in Streatham he had assembled one of the best private galleries in the country, mostly comprising of contemporary paintings, though fairly conservative in taste. He was a close friend of the Royal Academy's Director, Sir John Everett Millais and an encourager of young English artists. He had always intended to bequeath the collection to the nation but it became clear the National Gallery could not accept more than a fraction of his collection. After a lot of discussion the outcome was the establishment of a new gallery on the site of Millbank Prison. Henry Tate's initial contribution was £80,000 towards the building costs and sixty-five pictures from his personal collection. Of course, the Tate name has in more recent times been lent also to the small gallery in St Ives, the gallery (appropriately) situated alongside Liverpool's Albert Dock and London's *Tate Modern* on the South bank of the Thames.

Other examples of Tate's generosity in the London area included the establishment of a free library in his home area of Streatham and bequests for libraries in Balham, Lambeth and Brixton.

Ullet Road Church Hall, with the arms of Sir Henry Tate and Sir John Brunner above the fireplace.

What of Tate the man? From all accounts, for someone so able and energetic, he was surprisingly private and modest. His generous donations to the causes in which he believed were always made discreetly and often anonymously. He twice declined a knighthood and was only persuaded in 1898 (the year before he died) to accept a baronetcy when he was told a further refusal would be considered a snub to the royal family. Like notable Unitarians before him (the Gregs at Styal for example), he had a reputation for showing concern for the working conditions of his employees. He remained sympathetic to the Unitarianism of his upbringing throughout his life and, in addition to his contributions to Liverpool Unitarian causes mentioned earlier, he provided funding for the Unitarian College in

Manchester and also gave £10,000 for the library at Manchester College Oxford, the training grounds for many Unitarian ministers up to the present day.

Henry Tate's special contribution has long been recognized in what was for many years his home city. He was given the Freedom of the City in Liverpool in 1891 and a brass plate in the foyer of the Tate Hall in the University of Liverpool bears an inscription which reads

> Henry Tate, Merchant and Freeman of the City of Liverpool,
> accounting the Gain of Wisdom better than Fine Gold,
> built and furnished this Library as a Treasure House
> of Learning and for the Goodly Fellowship of Students, AD 1892

In Ullet Road Church Sir Henry is fittingly remembered by a splendid three-panelled memorial window commissioned by his fellow worshippers and made to a Burne-Jones design. Closer to the present day, just across the Mersey, in 2001 a blue plaque was unveiled on the site of Sir Henry's first shop at 42, Hamilton Street, Birkenhead. This was the starting point of what was to be a most successful career, the fruits of which were to be shared among many.

Further Reading

T. Jones, *Henry Tate, 1819–1899* (London 1960)

P. Chalmin [translated by E. Long-Michalke], *The making of a sugar giant: Tate and Lyle, 1859–1989* (London 1990)

A. Watson, *A hundred years of sugar refining: the story of Love Lane refinery, 1872–1972* (Liverpool, 1973)

SIR JOHN BRUNNER 1842 – 1919

Politician, Industrialist, Philanthropist and Educationalist

Len W. Mooney

Brunner's father came from Bulach, Switzerland, where he had partially trained as a Lutheran minister but decided to come to England in 1832 settling in Everton. He opened a school, St George's in Netherfield Road. He found Unitarianism much to his liking and due to his training was given the honorary title of Reverend. He married Margaret Curphey from the Isle of Man. John was their fourth child born on 8th February 1842. Regrettably his mother died in 1847. Two years later his father married Nancy Inman, a Unitarian lady who successfully ran a school in Birkenhead. She was a warm hearted and shrewd lady who soon brought order to running the household and the school. John claimed he learned management from her.

The family worshipped at Renshaw Street chapel where John heard the great Unitarian preachers such as Martineau, John Hamilton Thom and Charles Beard; their Unitarianism was the guiding influence for the rest of John's life.

John left his father's school aged 16 to work in a firm dealing with America. The Civil War proved disastrous and John needed another job. His elder brother, the chief engineer at Hutchenson's Chemical factory at Widnes, found him a post in the office. That the owner had been educated at St George's may have been a factor. In twelve years John had become the office manager, well experienced in the commercial side of the industry. He had married a Liverpool lady, Salome Davies and fathered six children. Salome died in 1874 leaving John with six young children. He hired Ethel Wyman from Kettering as a governess and married her a year later.

Partnership with Ludwig Mond

Also at Hutchenson's was Ludwig Mond, a skilled German chemical engineer who already had many patents to his name. In 1871 Mond asked Brunner to join him in starting a new factory to obtain soda from common salt using ammonia. This process was newly patented by Ernest Solvay A site at Winnington was purchased near the salt mines of Cheshire. On the site was Winnington Hall in which initially the partners with their families lived in separate wings. In 1891 the Brunners moved to Druids Cross in Liverpool (now demolished). In 1907 John and Ethyl moved south due to her ill health. They chose a house, Silverlands in Chertsey, Surrey. Ethyl died in 1910. During the years in Liverpool John rejoined Renshaw

Street Chapel and when the congregation moved to Ullet Road he performed the opening ceremony in 1899. Together with Henry Tate they paid the cost of the cloisters and the magnificent hall. Brunner alone paid for the outstanding painted ceiling in the library. Park Lane chapel also benefited from Brunners's help.

The partners received very favourable terms from Solvay which enabled the firm to flourish. Mond claimed "we are not making chemicals we are making money." In 1881 a company was formed with 30,000 shares; Brunner and Mond each had 6000 and were appointed managing directors for life which ensured they became

Detail of the library ceiling at Ullet Road showing the portrait of Sir John Brunner (unnamed, to the left of Aristotle and behind Pestalozzi) by Gerald Moira

rich men and the company was run as they wished; professionals being in charge of the day to day work.

The 1885 Reform Act evened out the population of parliamentary constituencies and formed new ones including Northwich. John was its MP for 25 years from 1885 with just one small break until 1910 when he retired from parliament. Among the many bills he supported were Home Rule for Ireland, Education Reform and compensation for subsidence although he knew the latter would be costly for his company. He had a strong belief in education for workers and the company paid for boys and apprentices to attend night school. The company supported the welfare of its employees in several ways. The twelve hour shift system was replaced by an eight hour one; a paid holiday week was introduced. A full medical care scheme was started which included "sick pay" even for the boys; the employees paid little, the major part of the cost was borne by the company. Sports facilities were provided. Houses for employees were built and let at a low rent.

Sir John Brunner and Education

Brunner considered that the penal system was too harsh on young offenders who were mostly uneducated; the school room not the reformatory was his solution.

He was very dissatisfied with the quality of the existing elementary schools especially as he realized that an educated workforce would be an asset to the company and the nation. To help improve the situation Brunner Mond built a school at Winnington in 1886 and another at Moulton in 1894. For Brunner better education for everyone became a crusade. He promoted and supported Education Bills in parliament but was always concerned that Dissenters were forced to pay through rates and taxes for small village church schools which did not accept Dissenters' religious views. His lifelong interest in education was not a self-interested charitable gesture but an earnest desire to improve society.

In an attempt to remedy this locally he built and personally paid for a school at Barnton in 1898, where there was already a church school. With his view on religious toleration he insisted they be non-denominational which became a matter of concern to the then Bishop of Chester and much correspondence followed. Very soon the new school at Barnton exceeded the old school in both pupil numbers and the standard of education. Following the 1902 Education Act the above three schools were handed over to the county authorities. Brunner also provided new buildings for the existing grammar school in Northwich and founded many scholarships. Even after 1902 he continued to contribute to local education by providing the Victoria Road schools in Northwich in 1907.

At Barnton the building still stands. A much-weathered inscribed tablet on a side gable reads:

This school was built for the use of the inhabitants of the neighbourhood
by Sir John Brunner… and this memorial stone was laid in July 1952

Now known as the Memorial Hall the building is used by the Barnton Parish Council as a Community Centre and Clinic. Brunner would have approved of this.

To encourage the workforce the company required boys to attend evening classes until they reached 17 years of age, which was extended to 19 years except for apprentices who studied until 21. In all cases the company paid the five shillings fee for students with good attendance records and added a further half crown as a reward.

By a series of acts, known at the Clarendon Code, passed by Parliament during the period 1661 - 1673, Protestant Dissenters, such as Unitarians, were excluded from civic offices and universities. Dissenters therefore set up their own academies offering a wider education than the old universities. One was the Warrington Academy where Joseph Priestley taught in the 1760s. As a Unitarian he was obliged to conduct his valuable pioneering scientific research outside the orbit of universities. As a result of this exclusion Unitarians were always at the forefront in promoting higher education. The restriction on Unitarians continued until the 1813 Trinity Act removed the penalties for impugning the Trinity.

In 1877 a meeting between the Liverpool Royal School of Medicine and the Association for the Promotion of Higher Education agreed "on the desirability of establishing a College in Liverpool". The Reverend Charles Beard the minister of Renshaw Street Unitarian Chapel was chairman of the Association; William Rathbone (VI) and George Holt, members of his congregation, were committee members. A Town's Meeting held in the Liverpool Town Hall unanimously supported the idea and a committee was formed to promote the proposal and to raise funds; £75,000 was needed. By their subsequent efforts Beard, Rathbone and Campbell Brown, head of the Medical School, must be regarded as the founding fathers of the college. By July 1880 £90,000 had been raised. A charter was granted on 18th October 1881 and the inaugural meeting held in St George's Hall on 14th January 1882. The first home of University College was the old Lunatic Asylum in Brownlow Hill.

John Brunner would naturally have had contact with Beard and Rathbone at Renshaw Street Chapel; indeed he wrote to Beard, who died in 1888, regretting he had not been able to persuade Mond to support the College. Brunner gave much support. In 1885 he contributed towards a chair of engineering; in 1891 he gave £10,000 to endow a chair of Economic Science in memory of his father and his son Sydney, a student at the college who had died the previous year; in 1896 he donated towards the cost of a metallurgical laboratory. The college developed rapidly aided by other Unitarians. Henry Tate, of sugar fame, son of a Unitarian minister, promised £5000 for a Day Training College for Teachers and George Holt gave £15,000 to endow a chair of Physiology.

Brunner was elected to the College Council in 1902 by which time University status had become desirable. By October that year £170,000 had been raised to support the University and a Charter was granted on 15th July 1903. Sir John and another Unitarian, James Alsop, a Liverpool solicitor, played a significant role in drafting the Charter. Probably their influence resulted in the clause which specified "that no religious test shall be imposed - and no Theological Teaching shall be given". This applied to staff and students; Beard had obtained a similar clause for the original college charter.

Sir John continued his support by endowing two further chairs, Physical Chemistry in 1904 and Egyptology in 1905. In 1909 he was appointed Pro-Chancellor, a position he held until 1918 a year before his death. A local newspaper described the appointment as "a fitting honour and acknowledgement of his great services". On 8th May 1909 an Honorary Degree of Doctor of Laws was awarded to Sir John by the University. It was customary on these occasions for the students to sing a verse after each award. For Brunner they sang: -

Here's a good second to non-er
In his robes a stun-stun-stunner
And we have to confess
We could scarcely guess
It was Brun-Brun-Brun-Brun-Brunner

Although Sir John was often irascible he also had a sense of humour and would have enjoyed the joke.

The University Arts Collection has two pictures of Sir John. The more famous one, by Augustus John RA, was presented to the University Club by his fellow members. It is a somewhat dark picture about which Brunner commented that it made him look corpulent but the gift shows the high esteem in which he was held. The second portrait by Arthur Hacker RA is more vibrant and colourful. Sir John is wearing the vivid scarlet robes of a Doctor of Laws.

Support for Unitarian institutions

Naturally Brunner also supported the colleges specifically allied to Unitarianism. He served as vice president of Unitarian College in Manchester from 1888 until his death, being president for the year 1898. He was also president of Manchester College, Oxford, for the period of 1911 - 1917. This college is the successor to previous Unitarian academies, namely Warrington (1756-1783), previously mentioned, which became Manchester (New) College in York (1803-1840), back

to Manchester (1840-1853), then to London (1853-1889) before finally settling in Oxford in 1889 where a portrait of Sir John, also by Arthur Hacker, hangs on the main staircase. The college, now named Harris Manchester, is a full college of the University.

Sir John appears to have enjoyed sitting for his portrait; in addition to the three mentioned above there are three more in the possession of the family. The Catalyst Museum, Widnes, has a small delightful eight inch high bronze statuette of Sir John relaxing in an armchair with his feet resting on an animal skin rug. The work is by C. C. Mellino and dated Paris 1906.

Sir John Brunner

John's philanthropy seemed unbounded. He provided two libraries for Northwich, the second after the first collapsed from subsidence; he gave the deeds of the large Naylor House to Middlewich as a community centre, he paid for the Runcorn Guildhall and another at Winsford. He was among the first to propose the Transporter link between Runcorn and Widnes, subscribing much money and guaranteed loans. Eventually he made over to Widnes Corporation his whole financial interest, about £60,000, a very large sum for that period.

Although resigned from parliament he was still politically active representing his fellow ratepayers in Chertsey by obtaining a seat on the Surrey Council. He saw that Labour would eventually overtake the Liberals. In the 1918 election he supported the local Labour party by chairing their meetings and helping financially. He disliked the Liberal - Conservative coalition.

He died on 1st July 1919 and his ashes were buried along side his wife's in the church yard adjacent to Silverlands. In its obituary the *Times* newspaper described him "as not far short of being the most powerful man in the country". The life size statues of Brunner and Mond were cleaned and moved to their present site in the factory grounds in 1995; the unveiling ceremony was performed by the then Duchess of Kent, a great grand daughter of Brunner.

Brunner Mond was the major company when four chemical manufacturers merged to form ICI in the 1920s.

Further Reading

Len W. Mooney, 'Sir John Brunner' (unpublished biography)

See also Len W. Mooney, *A Guide to Ullet Road Unitarian Church* (Liverpool 1996)

LAWRENCE REDFERN 1888 – 1967

Distinguished pastor and preacher

Elizabeth Alley

Lawrence Redfern was born on 27th December 1888 at Great Hucklow, Derbyshire where his father, Robert Stuart Redfern, was the Unitarian minister.

His ministry covered a period of over 46 years and yet Redfern served only three churches – the Octagon Chapel in Norwich, Ullet Road in Liverpool and the Unitarian Church in Bournemouth. His outstanding time at Ullet Road lasted 32 years from 1918 to 1950.

Redfern was not only a gifted preacher, but contributed to the wider Unitarian movement as a scholar and administrator.

In the pulpit his eloquent style was powerful and stirring. His sermons were not designed to promote controversy. His aim was to convey a sense of the ethical and spiritual. He spoke to his congregation through the spirit of worship and by reminding them of their calling as children of God.

Lawrence Redfern

He was firmly of the view that a church service is a service of worship and must above all be constructed to bring people into contact with the Eternal. He created impressive services which suited whatever occasion.

The following article draws heavily on the excellent memoir of Redfern compiled and edited by Alec R. Ellis.

The Liverpool Cathedral Controversy

While Redfern was minister in Liverpool he contributed significantly not only to the life of the local Unitarian Churches but also to that of the city itself.

The wide regard in which he was held was made evident when he was invited to preach in Liverpool Cathedral by the Dean on Assize Sunday in October 1931. The background to the invitation was the fact that Sir Sydney Jones was a member of Ullet Road's congregation and in 1929 had been appointed High Sheriff of Lancashire, inviting Redfern to be his Chaplain.

The tradition was that it was customary for the Chaplain or the High Sheriff to preach the sermon at the opening of the Assizes in Lancaster, Liverpool and Manchester when the justices of assize attended morning service at the cathedral or parish church.

During Redfern's year as Chaplain he didn't preach a sermon, although he usually read one of the lessons. The Dean in Liverpool, however, was greatly concerned at this omission. The declared ideal of the cathedral was that it 'should be above all sectional and divisive influences' and this mission was not being upheld.

After some time, on 22nd October 1931, Redfern was invited to preach the Assize sermon in the cathedral. It was attended by HM Judges of Assize at the opening of the Autumn Assizes. His sermon was completely uncontroversial.

Several weeks went by and the event seemed to have passed off without controversy in the Liverpool Diocese, but then Lord Hugh Cecil in London revealed his objections. His view was that by permitting a Unitarian minister to preach at a liturgical service in an Anglican cathedral the Dean and Bishop of Liverpool should be formally charged before the Convocation of York.

At the end of these matters the Dean wrote in a letter of apology to Redfern:

> No one who knows anything of the history of Liverpool can fail to recognise joyfully and gratefully the signal services to every department of our City's welfare rendered by your church. Its ministers and members have been among the greatest Christians of our country and have left an ineffaceable mark upon the spiritual, educational, social and philanthropic records of the past century.

Service to church and society

Redfern was a committed Unitarian but his outlook was also deeply Christian. The divisions within orthodox dogma saddened him as he revealed in his little book "Essential Christianity and the present religious situation". Having said that, he enjoyed the friendship of many churchmen and women whose faith differed widely from his own.

He had a profound belief that Unitarian churches were well placed to play a central part in the religious life of his times. He himself used his many talents in making a great variety of contributions to local, district and national organisations.

He travelled in pursuit of his Unitarian interests. In 1922 he was a member of an Anglo-American commission which visited the religious minorities in Transylvania and Romania. He was part of the British delegation to the USA in 1925 taking part in the commemoration of the centenary of both the British and Foreign Unitarian Association and the American Unitarian Association (each founded in 1825). He represented the General Assembly in 1937 on an official tour of Unitarian churches in Canada and Australia.

An engraving of the chancel of Ullet Road Church

While Redfern had prodigious gifts as a preacher and administrator his personality was attractive and vivacious. His wife, Eleanor Rhodes, MA, an intellectual equal from his undergraduate days at Manchester University, and their three sons formed a powerful family unit.

He was particularly renowned for his wit and infectious humour and was a brilliant after-dinner speaker. His humour, however, did not detract from his earnestness and dedication.

Many of Redfern's attributes were not obvious to the congregation when he preached his first service. He was impressive as a preacher - dignified, reverent and inspiring, but he would one day go on to win the Sefton Park singles tennis championship; he would become known throughout the City of Liverpool as a witty after-dinner speaker; and unwittingly cause ecclesiastical history by preaching in Liverpool Cathedral.

For 32 years at Ullet Road, Sunday by Sunday, his congregations experienced a plethora of emotions as they were inspired by sermons of the highest standard.

Redfern was lucky to have solid support throughout his ministry at Ullet Road from renowned Liverpool citizens. The Chairman of the congregation until his death, Sir Richard D. Holt, with Lady Holt, supported him in whatever way possible. Sir R.H. Armstrong, Pro-Chancellor of the University, on succeeding Sir Richard, continued this type of assistance.

The Rathbone Literary Club was one of the clubs linked to Ullet Road and Redfern became a keen member. The society was a select group from the intelligentsia of Liverpool. He arranged speakers which were of such a quality that the Club became well known for its intellectual appeal.

He also identified himself with the Liverpool hospitals' governing body and was at one time Chairman of the Royal Liverpool Children's Hospital in Myrtle Street.

Latter Days

An extract from Redfern's 25th anniversary sermon demonstrates his mature and reflective thinking:

> Our Free Christian Churches have tried a wonderful experiment and have sustained it with astonishing success. They have offered to their ministers a free pulpit, and have bidden them preach freely and fearlessly the truth, the whole truth and nothing but the truth. They have trusted their moral and spiritual integrity. They have bidden them preach out of the fullness of personal conviction and to minister out of the depths of personal affection.

As well as a preacher, Redfern was committed to his pastoral duties. Every member of his congregation, at some time or other, received a visit conducted with empathy and understanding so that patience and courage could be brought to bear on troubles.

During the exhausting years of the Second World War, Redfern even held an academic post - as tutor in Christian doctrine for his old college in Manchester, the Unitarian College.

In 1943 he was invited to be Principal of the College but he saw this as posing a difficult decision. He held the College in high regard because of his student days. To be Principal was tempting. But he felt the war was starting to turn and envisaged men returning with the expectation that Ullet Road and all it stood for would have survived. He decided he must be there to welcome them back.

Redfern did not move from Liverpool until 1950, his last ministry being at the Unitarian Church in Bournemouth.

He died on 17th April 1967 at Bournemouth at the home of one of his sons after some months of serious illness.

In a letter written to a friend on 8th January 1967, a few weeks before he died, he wrote these words:

> Time passes and reveals that we are all touched with mortality. But though the *things* for which we have affection are taken away, God leaves us the affection in perpetuity, and this is immortality.

Further Reading

Obituaries, *The Inquirer* 22nd April, 29th April, 6th May, 20th May, 3rd June (1967).

Lawrence Redfern A Memoir, compiled and edited by Alec R. Ellis (Bournemouth 1968).

The Triumph of Truth, the centrepiece of the library ceiling at Ullet Road Church,
painted by Gerald Moira

SIR ADRIAN BOULT 1889 – 1983

Eminent 20th century conductor

Richard Merritt

Adrian Boult – the formative years

One of England's most famous conductors was brought up in the Liverpool city region in the 1890s and had important links to the city at later stages of his life. Adrian Boult, although actually born in Chester in 1889, moved to Brooke House in Blundellsands, a popular commuting suburb at that time, before he was two. His father, Cedric, was another of those successful Liverpool Unitarian businessmen, well-to-do, but altruistic. He was an oil merchant and, although the family home was relatively plain and unostentatious compared with many, the family's wealth meant that Adrian and his younger sister Olive could be brought up in the English upper-middle class style. The house had a billiards room and quarters for the servants. Adrian was provided with a good education and could afford to attend concerts in his formative years. At one stage he was paying six guineas an hour for conducting advice (from Landon Ronald), which in 1915 was an enormous sum for tuition!

The Boult family had been Unitarian going back at least 100 years, and there were Boults buried in Chester's Matthew Henry Chapel in the early 1800s. When Adrian's family moved to West Kirby when Adrian was 15 the Boults were founder members of the Unitarian church there, and Adrian is said to have helped on the musical side when home during the school holidays. When the Boults moved to London after the First World War he attended the old Unitarian Chapel in Great Portland Street where his parents had been married. He was himself later to be married in a Unitarian church. Although he never lived in Chester again Adrian was nominally a member of Chester's Matthew Henry Chapel up to the time he died at the grand old age of 93 in 1983.

Boult was a precocious little boy. From the age of eight months he reacted to music and would stop what he was doing when he heard it. The young Boult would listen to his mother at the piano and have a little go himself. By the age of four, without having been taught, he was playing simple things with two hands, putting in a bass harmony, was playing things alternatively in the major then the minor key just for fun, and seemed to know the musical notes without having been taught them, much to his mother's surprise. Prominent people including musicians came to the house from time to time - people like composer Hubert Parry for example.

At the age of five he went to his first concert, a recital give by a baritone in Liverpool. By the age of six he was writing little compositions, knew his scales on the piano up to five flats and went to his first orchestral concert at the Philharmonic Hall Liverpool. Hans Richter was touring with his London Orchestra and in his parents' box he listened to Wagner's *Siegfried Funeral March* and loved it. This had been included to respect Sir Charles Hallé who had died in Manchester the previous day. Here he heard for the first time a full symphony, Tchaikovsky's

Sir Adrian Boult

6th, the *Pathétique*. In his parents' box he was trying to beat time to conduct the music and was apparently only temporarily confused by the 5/4 rhythm in the second movement.

When he was seven he was taken to *Tannhauser* and the *Flying Dutchman* but alongside this he had the interests of other children. As he got older, at one stage golf took his fancy, not surprising living, as he was, near the home of West Lancashire Golf Club, one of the ten oldest golf clubs in the country, and the oldest in Lancashire.

But music was the "big thing" and by the time he was eleven he was quite knowledgeable about a wide range of music. At the age of 12 he was sent to Westminster School in London where one of the masters taught him analysis. At weekends he went to Henry Wood's Saturday and Sunday concerts. But it was hearing Nikisch conduct Wagner and Tchaikovsky in 1902 that made him decide at the age of 12 that he wanted to be a conductor. Boult noticed how Nikisch produced a completely different sound from the orchestra throwing a totally different light on the music. So he was spurred to learn more about music and bought scores with his pocket money, sang in Westminster Abbey on occasion, continued to write his own music and analysed the works of the great composers.

It was when Boult was fifteen that he first heard Elgar's *Dream of Gerontius* in what was actually only its second public performance. Given he was later to play it many times and also produce a recording (considered one of the very best) his views on the work as a fifteen-year old are somewhat condescending. "I was very disappointed. It is a very aimless wandering. The closing scene is exquisite and the demon chorus is good but Gerontius takes too long dying although phrases are lovely. Will Elgar live? His *Variations* will I am certain. Will *Gerontius*? I am not certain by any means."

He did concede that the poor quality of the performance may have led to a lot of it being "deadly dull." However half a year later he heard the work for the second time and conceded "the whole idea and carrying out of the words is magnificent and to me the deadly dull parts are much fewer and further between. His treatment of orchestra and chorus is excellent all through."

Boult was 16 when he first met Elgar through a friend Frank Schuster who he had got to know through an old lady he used to visit when in Blundellsands who according to Boult was lovable but formidable and modelled herself on Queen Victoria! Later in life Elgar had reason to be grateful to Boult for promoting his music when it was going out of fashion with the public. But when Boult was at Birmingham in the Twenties he once suggested a scaling down of resources in a performance of *Gerontius* and Elgar took the huff. Seven years later when Elgar was to celebrate his 75th birthday, relations were restored. It clearly was an interesting relationship; on one occasion Boult was reputed to have said "If Elgar's music is played badly you blame the orchestra; if it played well you blame Elgar."

After Westminster School, Adrian went to Christ Church, Oxford where he eventually gained a doctorate. In 1912 he entered Leipzig Conservatory. He should have waited two years before joining the conducting class but was allowed to do so after just six weeks. His main reason for going there however was to go to Nikisch's rehearsals and learn from his example. 1913 saw Boult helping at Covent Garden amongst all his other activity.

The Liverpool connection was not completely severed; he was still returning home to his family on a regular basis, and Adrian's first professional concert as a conductor was with a group of Liverpool Philharmonic players in West Kirby's Public Hall on 1914, when he was 24. It was an ambitious programme and he was warned in particular that the *Italian Serenade* by Wolf was a difficult piece. At the rehearsal the wind soloist came in a bar late and Boult told him so. The wind player said "I've played this work a hundred times and I know I was right". Boult said "Very Well Mr X <u>we</u> were <u>all</u> a bar early." a remark which led to cheers from the orchestra. The *Liverpool Daily Post* critic said

the conductor was well-read in his scores, appears at all times to have control over his instrumental forces under him and the ability to impart here and there a delicate touch or to proceed to a bold effective climax. Amidst all this – perhaps it is the most thankful point of all – his manner is devoid of all ostentation.

Later in 1914 war broke out. Musicians in the Hallé and Liverpool Philharmonic were having a bad time, people were stopping taking lessons and there were fewer concerts. Times were hard. Boult, with his father's help (as the public-spirited, Unitarian businessman he was) organized some concerts in Liverpool using some 30 people from the Liverpool Philharmonic. He hired the Sun Hall in Kensington, Liverpool and charged low prices - between 2d and 2/6, playing popular works on Friday evenings. Initially things were a bit slow but after the first four concerts he then put on further concerts in the David Lewis Club in Great George Place, made available through an old family friend, Frederick Marquis. Frederick was in charge of the University Settlement, a club run by the University for dockers; later he was to be managing director of Lewis's and eventually became the prominent politician Lord Woolton. Gradually Boult included less popular works in the concerts but despite this audiences gradually increased to around 1000. Added to this, he got a good press as conductor.

During the war Boult did a fair bit of what he called "amateur soldiering" for five hours a day drilling King's (Liverpool) Regiment recruits who were billeted at the same Public Hall in which he had given his first professional concert. But his involvement in the war beyond that was tempered by his health which was at times borderline. He had been taken ill with a bad heart the year before, after singing in Wagner's *Parsifal*. He did later in the war get the chance to help in the War Office, partly in translating the German press, having learned German a year or so before (and started life with a German nurse – according to his mother his first utterances as a toddler were in German).

In 1916, based on the concerts he had been putting on in Liverpool, to Boult's surprise and delight the Liverpool Philharmonic itself asked him to conduct a concert for them as guest conductor. The involvement of a refugee from the Antwerp Opera and the inclusion of the Belgian National Anthem reflected the wartime context. The famous Solomon was the piano soloist. The *Musical Standard* commented, "the programme revealed the catholicity of his musical tastes and his ability to interpret widely differing schools. His lead is clear and convincing if somewhat lacking in that magnetism which holds in a relentless grip both orchestra and audience. There is no doubt that this musician is destined to do much in the cause of native orchestral composition."

Boult commented in his autobiography "the Royal Liverpool Philharmonic Society...has remembered me almost continuously since, and I have many happy memories of their concerts." Boult later in his life accompanied the cellist Pablo Casals at Liverpool and took the BBC Symphony Orchestra there in 1950, but a particular memory of the Liverpool Philharmonic was as a young man attending rehearsals whenever he was at home from school or University. He considered this a valuable privilege. When the Czech conductor Talich conducted in Liverpool Boult helped on the translation side.

Another connection with Liverpool was Boult's acquaintance with Gordon Stutely, first violin in the Liverpool Philharmonic Orchestra who was also Conductor of the Liverpool City Police Band. He was an expert on every instrument in the band and had access to the instruments. Boult gradually learned from him the fingering and embouchure of the various band instruments sufficient at least to blow a few notes on each.

During the war years, helped by a reference from the Liverpool Philharmonic Society Board, he got the chance to organize four Queen's Hall concerts in London specifically to encourage English music. He became friendly with Gustav Holst around this time. At times the concerts had to compete with Zepellin raids. His conducting of the Vaughan Williams *London Symphony* was generally acclaimed and Vaughan Williams himself wrote to Boult saying "It really was splendid; you had got the score right into you and through you into your orchestra. May I say how much I admired your conducting – it is real *conducting* – you get just what you want and *know* what you want and your players trust you because they know it also…"

Boult and *The Planets*

So it was perhaps not surprising that shortly before the end of the war Holst asked him to conduct the first performance of his recently completed suite *The Planets*.

The performance went very well and Holst said that Boult had "covered himself with glory" in playing the work – and that he was the "the first to make the Planets shine in public." However he obviously didn't think the interpretation was perfect and had some hints for Boult when he came to perform the second performance. Regarding *Mars the Bringer of War* Holst wrote "You made it wonderfully clear, now could you make more **row**. And work up more sense of climax. Perhaps hurry certain bits. Anyway it must sound more unpleasant and far more terrifying." Boult seems to have taken Holst's advice to heart and describing Boult's second performance of *Mars* the *Times* said it was " as bad an exhibition of frightfulness as the modern orchestra can produce."

Because of his relatively reserved conducting style there was always a danger that audiences might feel he lacked commitment, but evidence suggests this was not the case. A member of the London Philharmonic Orchestra told Michael Kennedy (Boult's biographer) that when Boult was conducting *Mars*, from the back (the audience's view) he hardly seemed to be moving. But the orchestral musicians, facing the conductor, could see that he was almost foaming at the mouth! Boult was later to record the *Planets* five times and at the time of writing his final recording is still considered one of the very best by the *Gramophone* in its CD guide.

Early conducting career and the Birmingham Symphony Orchestra

After the war in 1918 he conducted two concerts for the Royal Philharmonic Society and started providing conducting classes at the Royal College of Music. In 1919 he was conducting for the Russian Ballet with Diaghilev.

At this stage Boult had clearly "arrived" as a conductor. Yet his original ambition to conduct opera had been somewhat overtaken by other things. Already he was seen as someone enmeshed in the work of the College and promoting the cause of English music. In 1920 he became conductor of the British Symphony Orchestra, set up from ex-serviceman musicians; he struggled to make a go of the orchestra after its manager went bankrupt. Boult felt he could have succeeded if he had had more time to devote to the management side. But at this time he was doing many other things and this included the first performance of Vaughan Williams's *Pastoral Symphony* and Bliss's *Colour Symphony* (dedicated to Boult).

Boult visited Toronto and the United States and while he was there was offered the position of conductor of the Philharmonic Orchestra in Rochester, New York State, where there is now a large Unitarian congregation in a notable modernistic building. Whether Boult met fellow Unitarians while over there is not recorded but he was certainly tempted to accept the offer and apparently had his bags packed to make the trip back there.

However, when Sir Henry Wood resigned from the Birmingham Festival Choral Society, he turned his back on America and took on the Birmingham job even though the reason for Sir Henry's resignation was stated to be the poor prevailing orchestral conditions. His biographer speculates on why he turned down an easier life in a wealthy city in the United States and puts it down to the fact he had had in some respects a charmed life already, always having had the support of his well-to-do parents. Kennedy suggests that his musical activities had often shown him to be socially conscious and that it was in his character to stay and build something in England rather than go to a ready-made orchestra in America.

So it was that Boult became conductor of the Birmingham Festival Choral Society in 1923 and by 1924 he was in charge also of the City of Birmingham Orchestra (now the CBSO) as its second ever conductor. He was there for six seasons during which time he also carried out much guest conducting in Britain and abroad; he also at this time conducted the Bach Choir. One commentator said of the way he had improved the Birmingham orchestra "I do not believe that there is anyone else living in England with that rare combination of musicianship and character which enabled you to lift us out of the slough in which we were wallowing and set us on our feet. If the orchestra has any success in the future we shall not forget that it is only you who have made it possible"

One of his guest appearances of this time was in Liverpool to conduct *Parsifal*, the *Liverpool Daily Post* finding it "a very sensitive and restrained treatment of the orchestral score…the playing was singularly homogenous and impressive."

At this stage Boult had matured to become what he was to be for the rest of his life: very capable but not particularly charismatic. Kennedy says "whatever may have constituted the general public's idea of a conductor, it was not Boult. He could not rival the characterful avuncular popularity of Wood, he had none of Beecham's raffish charm and devilry; he lacked the brilliance and panache of Sargent; he had not the magnetic intensity of Barbarolli. Even his appearance was against him; with his baldness, his full moustache and formal dress he looked more like a country solicitor than a musician. His courteous manner seemed even then slightly old fashioned." A friend said of him, he was born at the age of 40.

Boult at the BBC

But, charisma or not, Boult was the man chosen to become Director of Music at the BBC in 1929 and Boult conducted the first concert of the new BBC Symphony Orchestra. Critics talked of the best English orchestral playing since the war, a fine conductor and sensitive musician having returned to London, and the "exquisite opening to *Daphne and Chloe*". A critic in *The Sackbut* wrote "If a *great* conductor is a person who reveals hidden beauties in well-known works, who never gets between you and the music, whose conception of a work is not of a point to point race but of a carry through, knowing the perfect moment for a climax, and having the ability to get it from his orchestra, then I should say Adrian Boult was that much abused word – *great*."

This was a period in which the BBC promoted new works. Although Boult gained a reputation for championing English works, his position at the BBC led to his conducting many new works from both English and non-English composers. First performances, or first performances in England, included, amongst others, works by Berg, Hindemith, Milhaud, Khachaturian, William Schuman, Kabalevsky, Tippett, Stravinsky, Martinu, Samuel Barber, Britten, Lutyens, Copland, Elizabeth Maconchy, Simpson, Shostakovitch, Hoddinott and fellow Unitarian, Béla Bartók. At this period of his career Boult had a regular radio series "Music of the Week" which included subjects like "Choosing New Music" and "Welcome to Casals."

In 1933 Boult carried out what he called the performance of his life – ie. he got married to Ann Wilson, a divorcée. This was a quiet affair with only a dozen people there and was carried out at the Unitarian Old Meeting House, Ditchling, East Sussex, where Walford Davies played the harmonium for the occasion. They had a picnic on the Downs afterwards. The quietness of the occasion was quite typical of Boult who, although rather formal and used to being with famous people, wasn't a showy person at all and tended to shy away from the limelight when he could.

Coming back to Boult's career, there were times when competition between the BBC and Beecham (who ran the LPO) was rather hectic. Boult couldn't get on with Beecham. They were chalk and cheese, Boult prim and proper and inclined to be serious, Beecham rather devious and liking to rock the boat. On the other hand he got on well with, and admired, Toscanini who in turn was very complimentary about the quality of the BBC Symphony Orchestra under Boult. Boult saw Toscanini as someone to learn from - though his attempts to memorize scores like Toscanini did not really succeed. He concluded that "Toscanini's method is a law unto itself, not applicable to smaller fry"

But although Boult saw himself as "small fry" he was himself appreciated and in 1937 was knighted and later in the year asked to conduct the orchestral music before and after George VI's coronation service. In the late 1930s just before the war Boult carried out much guest conducting abroad which included the first Viennese performance of the *Variations for Orchestra* by the Viennese composer Schoenberg. The reaction in Vienna was mild horror, the President asking Boult "who is this composer Schoenberg anyway?!" presumably forgetting he was Vienna's most famous contemporary composer.

When war broke out in 1939, the BBC decamped first to Bristol and then to Bedford. During the war Boult also conducted some concerts in London in between the raids and also in the other British cities including Manchester and again in his original home area, Liverpool.

After the war Boult was the first foreigner to conduct the Concertgebouw Orchestra in Amsterdam and the Choral Society commissioned a performance of *The Dream of Gerontius* in English as a *thank you* to Britain. Boult did lots of touring at this stage and managed to get at least one English work into most programmes. And in London in 1946 he conducted Berg's *Wozzeck* for the second time having conducted the first complete British performance earlier in his career.

Hope Street Church, which stood next to
the Philharmonic Hall

In this post-war period he began to support the Federal Union promoting federalism as an alternative to nationalism for the future harmony of the world. He became its Vice-President soon after joining the movement. He also became President of the National Youth Orchestra having supported its establishment when some musicians did not favour the idea.

In 1942 Bliss took on some of Boult's administrative duties as BBC Music Director which enabled him to concentrate even more on the conducting side. Boult did some important recordings with EMI in the late 1940s including Vaughan Williams's *Job* , Holst's *Planets* and Elgar's Cello Concerto with his friend Pablo Casals. In 1942 Boult conducted *Gerontius* in Liverpool and in 1947 Boult was awarded an honorary Doctor of Laws at the University of Liverpool.

It was supposed to be a BBC rule that employees retire by age 61 but Boult had been more or less promised there would be an extension and wanted to improve the quality of the BBC orchestra which had suffered through the war. Things were rather awkward since the new Head of Music from 1948 was his wife's previous husband with whom he had an uneasy relationship. The upshot was that after much negotiating and "argy bargy" Boult had to leave on the basis he had reached the age of 61 though he felt he was effectively sacked.

After the BBC

As it happened, the departure from the BBC did not turn out too badly. He was only out of work for three or four days having been offered the prestigious job as Music Director of the London Philharmonic. There began an important association, and now in his 60s Boult started a new successful chapter in his musical life.

In 1953 he conducted at a coronation for the second time, that of Queen Elizabeth II.

After a trip to Russia which he had tried unsuccessfully to avoid (Russia had indicated his not being there with the orchestra would be a snub) in 1956 Boult gave notice of his wish to step down as musical director at the LPO, though he was effectively still in charge until 1959 and links with the orchestra lasted longer than that.

The rest of Boult's career was characterized by guest conducting and many forays into the recording studio. The first golden disc awarded by EMI for selling a million records was to the Beatles but the second was to Sir Adrian Boult. At this time he recorded all the Vaughan Williams symphonies with the composer present. In 1965 he conducted the RLPO in Liverpool, and again in 1969 where the venue was Chester Cathedral. This concert was special for Boult since his godchild, Hester Dickson, was playing the Mozart B flat piano concerto with the orchestra: "as she has lost two husbands after nursing sad and difficult illnesses I feel I would like to do all I can to help her now she is a real professional again." At this stage of his career Kennedy writes of Boult "he was becoming that much-loved institution, a 'character.' Never one to court the limelight, repelled by any suggestion of 'showmanship' his very modesty and reticence were now being seen as virtues which caught the public eye."

Boult's conducting style

What of Boult's style of conducting and arranging the orchestra? Boult believed that the baton should be an extension of the arm and one should not use two arms to beat time. He did not favour over demonstrative waving of the arms. He believed strongly that the conductor should not come between the listener and the music.

Boult had some strong views on the arrangement of the orchestra. For example he felt it was important that the conductor should not stand between soloists and the audience – this was something that used to happen at one time. Also Boult used to place the first violins at one side of the orchestra and the seconds on the other side. The usual plan is to start at the left with first violins, then radiating to the right the second violins, then violas, then cello, then double bass. Boult has commented on this arrangement, "this plan puts all the treble on the left and all the bass on the right and I submit gives the audience a most unbalanced picture of the orchestral sound. Those sitting on the right of the hall (facing the platform) will get a preponderance of bass; in fact in the Royal Festival Hall if one sits on that side one hears the bass sound first, and the tunes trickle across the hall a fraction late." He also has argued that the seconds need to be as prominent as the first, not tucked behind, especially important in "give and take" passages which have occurred in much music from Mozart onwards.

He didn't believe in over rehearsal of works before concerts saying "I feel that staleness is a thing that is very much neglected and much overlooked. A great many of my colleagues don't notice when their stuff is getting stale. It's as bad as that. This modern habit of having a rehearsal on the afternoon of the concert is to me a great mistake and I always resist it if I can. If I've got to do it I put as much rehearsal into the day before to avoid having much to do on the day of the concert."

Boult conducted the more mainstream works from memory but always had the score there on the desk. The composer

Matthew Henry's Chapel Chester

Derek Bourgeouis says of his experience at college attending Boult's conducting lessons: "Sir Adrian Boult was very dictatorial about conducting. He hated students who spoke too much and urged us all to say everything with the point of the stick rather than waste time talking in rehearsals. He was always very complimentary to me but tore other students to shreds in a very forthright way if they wanted to do things differently. However, for those prepared to play along with his methods there was a huge amount of wisdom to be gleaned."

An admirer describes his style thus:

> His composure and his subtle hand motions had a sort of dignified manner. He personified Englishness. He looked kind of elegant in his black suit: a tall man, typically not moving that much and sometimes slightly leaning ahead - like curving himself in a humble manner - with his left hand waving gently through an imposing sense of control. Boult inherited his 'style' from legendary conductors such as Richter, Wood or Nikisch. When Boult is finished, you always feel you understand what the piece is about. His technique was quite efficient even if at times it might have looked somewhat diffident or a little bumbling.

Finally…

Overall Boult was quite a content sort of person who worked hard, enjoyed learning, recognized his duty and responsibilities, put the music before personal showmanship, and to some extent just got on with things.

He was asked "Looking back over the years is there anything that has really perturbed you in the musical world?" He answered thus:

> No, I don't think I can say. I'm not that sort of person, you see. I just take things as they come and do my best to make the best of them. I have my likes and dislikes, of course, but further than that I don't think I can honestly go.

Boult wasn't formally to retire until 1981 when he was 92, very much the grand old man of British music. The last music he heard was Vaughan Williams *Sea Symphony*. He went to sleep in the middle of it and died the following day. Appropriate he should hear this music last when he had done so much to promote the music of English composers, including Vaughan Williams himself.

Acknowledgments

Although avoiding the use of copious bibliographic references, this short life of Sir Adrian Boult draws heavily from the sources set out in the concluding bibliography (below), and in particular acknowledgement is made of the author's liberal use of Michael Kennedy's excellent biography.

Further Reading

Michael Kennedy, *Adrian Boult* (Hamish Hamilton, London 1987)

Sir Adrian Boult, *My Own Trumpet* (Hamish Hamilton, London 1973)

Sir Adrian Boult, *Boult on Music* (Toccata Press, Gloucester 1983)

Jerrold Northrop Moore (ed.), *Music & Friends: letters to Sir Adrian Boult* (Hamish Hamilton, London 1979)

Robert Chesterman (ed.), *Conversations with conductors* (Robson Books, London 1976)

THE VISITORS' BOOK OF THE ANCIENT CHAPEL

As one of the most historic places of worship in Liverpool the Ancient Chapel attracts many visitors and a book preserves the names of many of them

Bernard Cliffe

The visitors' book of the Ancient Chapel is of some interest. The book at present in use was opened on 22nd May 1932 with an entry recording the visit of Clara L. Wilson, whose address was Clover, St John's Road, Knutsford, followed by an entry for Donald Evison McGregor, of Edinbro, Midlothian. The street name is given, but is written in a style which is rather difficult to make out. Between this date, and the beginning of the war there were just over three hundred entries, some of which represented a family rather than an individual.

Few of our visitors wrote any message about their visit to the chapel, but a number have made it clear that they wished to be known.

The names of some of our visitors are immediately recognizable as having a connection with the chapel. There are likely to be the names of others whose connections with the chapel are now not so obvious, but who were perhaps well known at the time of their visit. On 24th October 1933 is noted the visit of "Margaret Evelyn Arbuthnot, great, great granddaughter of the Rev John Yates, great granddaughter of his son Joseph Barford Yates, whose eldest daughter, Elizabeth married Samuel H. Thompson of Thingwall, Broad Green, whose second daughter Margaret married Herbert Mortimer Luckock in Childwall Church, 1866, who were her parents."

On 21st October 1932, Frank L. Cook, of Bahia Blanca, Argentina, visited the chapel. On 6th April 1936, is an entry for V.D. Davies, who was minister from 1883 to 1894. Dorothy R. Watkins (Odgers) and Margaret Odgers visited the chapel in the same year. James Edwin Odgers was minister from 1878 to 1882.

Visits were made by representatives of other chapels, including Old Meeting House, Coseley, Stourbridge Unitarian Church, Toxteth Congregational Chapel, Gee Cross Chapel, Kingswood Chapel, Hollywood, and Netherend, Staffordshire.

One of our American visitors was Mary Scott-Simpson, Superintendent of Joseph Priestley House. Another entry which catches the eye was made on 29th July 1934 by George Eyre Evans, the Liverpool-born Unitarian historian and antiquary, who wrote in green ink, after his name, "who first worshipped here in January, 1874."

A.L. Stimm, Guide Leader, accompanied seven members of her troop, each of whom wrote by name 'G.G.' All gave addresses in the area of Lance Lane.

Ancient Chapel

Visitors to the chapel had travelled from many parts of the British Isles, including a lady from Jersey. There were visitors from Berne, from Murcia, from Transylvania and from Denmark. One traveller had arrived from Jerusalem, Palestine. A surprising number had come from Australia, South Africa, one from Colombo, Ceylon and one from Singapore. There were travellers from the United States, mostly from Massachusetts, including Manchester by the Sea, and King's Chapel, Boston, but also from Pennsylvania and California. A number of people had travelled from Toronto and British Colombia. It seems surprising that travellers were able to make long journeys at a time of great financial difficulty for so many people in all countries.

Our Visitors' Book is now rather battered, but still in use. It has been well thumbed, so that a number of entries, particularly at the lower corners of pages, are illegible. I remembered as I prepared this that these people had no ball-point pens, which became available only after the end of the war. Those who carried one would have taken out their fountain pens, while the others used a pencil. The chapel does not seem to have had pen and ink to hand. Even now, although we make the effort, a ball-point pen is not always to be found with the book.

During the war the chapel continued to welcome visitors. On 3rd January 1940 we have the name of a visitor from Hungary, but unfortunately it cannot be read. On 9th May 1940 the chapel was visited by Ralph and Alice Atkinson of Pasadena,

California. The next day the German onslaught on France and the Low Countries began. I wonder whether these travellers were able to return to their home countries, or whether they were stranded by the war.

In the war years people were urged by the government to have Holidays at Home, presumably to reduce demand for rail and bus services by non-essential users. In any case, many beaches had been mined and covered with barbed wire. The Liverpool Show was staged at Wavertree, and at that time it provided an opportunity for allotment holders, then engaged in a Dig for Victory campaign, to display their produce, and compete for certificates. My father was the happy recipient of several of these. As well as receiving visitors from Merseyside, the chapel was visited by people from further afield in the UK. There are addresses in Kirkham, Fleetwood, Preston, Staffordshire, Essex, London and Birmingham. On 26th April 1944 A.D. Kay from Australia, accompanied by F.G. Dixon of Huyton, recorded a visit. A serviceman on leave, perhaps. In March 1945 W.R. Muskett of West Englewood, New Jersey, entered his name in our book. For some servicemen and women the war may well have given a once in a lifetime opportunity to make a visit.

In the years immediately following the end of the war there were few entries of any kind. Travel remained difficult and rather uncomfortable for a time. By 1948 the number of home and overseas visitors began to increase, and the entries between then and now number over 2,500. In 1968 an exhibition was held at the chapel to mark its 350th anniversary, and of the visitors more than 280 wrote their names. Many had come from Merseyside, but a considerable number had travelled a greater distance, and I have wondered how the organizers got the publicity. Since 1997 we have taken part in the National Heritage weekend each September, and still attract more than a hundred visitors each year.

People visit the chapel for a number of reasons. A remark frequently made, and sometimes written in our book, is that they had often passed by, and wondered what it was like inside. In 2003 Rita McEvoy wrote "have lived here for many years and have always wanted to see around. Most impressed." M. Grey wrote "wanted to visit for years. Very pleased I've made it." Debbie Lang from the Dingle wrote in 2004, "Standing at the bus stop always wanted to come and have a look around."

Other visitors had been members of the congregation in their youth, and recalled those days with pleasure. On the Heritage Day of 2005 Sue Shannon of Wigan wrote, "Came to Brownies here as a child." One very wet afternoon recently Mike and Mavis Brown saw that the door was open and asked to see around. Mike had been in the congregation as a boy, and wrote, "Happy memories as an ex-scout member 1952-53." In the meeting room he had taken his first steps on the stage in a life-long career in amateur dramatics. We realized that my family had seen him on occasion in pantomime. We were able to put him in touch with the Rev Dr Philip

Tindall, who had been minister at the time. Recently we in the congregation had the pleasure of sending greetings to Dr Tindall on the occasion of his 90th birthday.

Anna Jackson wrote, "Lovely to see inside at long last. V interesting," while Thelma Cornwell wrote, "Fascinating." Sometimes we have people who wish to enquire about members of their families whose lives may be recorded in the chapel baptismal or burial registers, dating from the 1780s, or in the marriage register, which was begun about one hundred years later. Many seek graves, but it is unfortunate that weathering has made some stones difficult or even impossible to read. Often, however, ours is not the church in question. One lady asked about the grave of a returned soldier who had been awarded the Croix de Guerre during the First World War. I felt sure that I would have remembered having read of such a rare distinction, but although I looked I could find no trace. There is some confusion arising from names. The cemetery in Smithdown Road is more correctly called Toxteth Cemetery, while a number of churches in our area have the word Toxteth in their names.

In July 2002 Scott and Jane Bowring of Exeter called on us as they wished to see the grave of a child in their family. In 2001 Rob and Ann Roberts wrote of their connection with the Harvey family, some of whose graves lie in the Old Ground, nearest the chapel – "antecedents buried here, and my parents (Hannay and Bowring) married here 5th of June 1940. Thank you for opening for us." At the same time there was a message from Patricia A.S. Sparacino – "Antecedents (Harvey) buried here. A lovely church. San Mateo, California, USA."

From time to time we receive visits from people whose family members have served the chapel. On one of our open days John Pike came to the chapel but we were not made aware of this until after he had left. He is the grandson of the Rev Frank Hemming Vaughan, who was minister from 1928 to 1943. On our open day

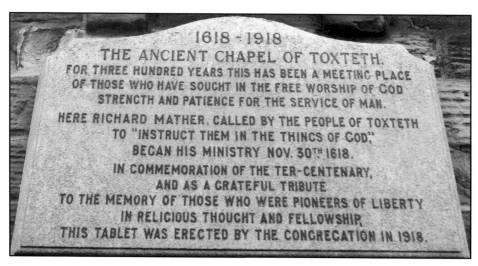

Tercentenary Commemorative Tablet

in 2006 Jane Moore called. Her great-grandparents had been caretakers in the 1920s. Other visitors are engaged in academic research. Several people have wished to examine the eighteenth century clock made by William Lassell. Tinho da Cruz of the University of Liverpool's cartographic department wished to photograph the grave of Richard Horwood. Before this I had not understood that Richard Horwood was a leader in the field of making street maps. The BBC have made a number of visits, the most recent being in connection with the memorial to Jeremiah Horrocks, on the occasion of the recent transit of Venus.

Handwriting is something of a problem. Some of it is unreadable, and I wonder why people do not make more of their visit. Others leave no doubt that they wish to be known, including my own grandson, David, who was then ten years old, and identified himself very clearly. One woman needed six lines. Some of the writing is a joy to read, and perhaps the most outstanding in this respect, is, I think, that of Noel R. Ellick, who came twice. His was a most beautiful copperplate hand. Some parents have obviously guided the hands of very young children, and I have been touched by their desire to record the occasion. Many of the comments are of great interest. The saddest was, perhaps, that of Mrs Lythgoe, of the Elms, a street very near to the chapel. She wrote on Remembrance Day 2002 "Twice a year." For some years she had brought flowers to the chapel in memory of her husband, but I am sorry that she has not called in recent years.

But what about this from Sam Riding on the Heritage Day of 2000? "BOOYAKUSHA - wicked 'tis rockin' I rate dis place." In spite of having made enquiries, I have only a vague idea of the drift of his meaning. I think he was pleased.

It has been a great pleasure for us to meet so many interesting people, and to share with them our beautiful chapel.

St Catherine's Church, Temple Court. Lithograph by W.G. Herdman 1843. The church was built by dissenters as the Octagon Chapel in 1763. Nicholas Clayton was appointed minister to a congregation made up of members of Key Street and Benn's Garden who gathered for worship with their own specially devised liturgy. It closed in 1776 and was demolished in 1819.

CONTRIBUTORS

Elizabeth Alley (née Bartlett) attended Stalybridge Unitarian Church as a child – her parents Rev Charles and Josephine Bartlett. Moved to Cross Street, Manchester, then various homes until settled with her own family in Liverpool, latterly attending Ullet Road Unitarian Church. The Bartlett connection coming full circle as Charles was born here, attended Ullet Road and was in the choir while Rev Laurence Redfern preached. He must have inspired young Bartlett to become a Unitarian minister. For myself really proud to attend church in such a beautiful complex of buildings, and with such a fantastic history of Unitarian witness.

Annette Butler. I was born in Gloucestershire, and was introduced to Unitarianism by my then neighbour Dr Stanley Kennett, a life-long Unitarian, as was his wife Millie. I started attending Ullet Road Church, Liverpool from late 1989. In recent years I became caretaker at Ancient Chapel of Toxteth which, like Ullet Road, is a Grade I listed building. Both are very remarkable places with a considerable history, shared with an appreciative public each National Heritage weekend every September. During my years in Ullet Road's congregation I have developed an interest in Gerald Moira, the muralist artist of the library and vestry, and continue to research him.

Bernard Cliffe. I was born in Liverpool and, apart from five or so years as a student and National Serviceman, I have lived all my life in the city. I came to Unitarianism about twenty years ago, and eventually settled at the Ancient Chapel, where I was welcomed by the congregation. I have spent a large part of my time since then in the exploration of the fascinating history of the chapel and its people, and in presenting it to our many visitors.

Rev John Keggen. Liverpool born of Celtic origin (Welsh and Manx). Unitarian minister for over forty years. Has held ministries at Gorton (Manchester), Gateacre and Hope Street, the Manx Fellowship, the Somerset and Dorset Group, and Chester and West Kirby. He currently serves as minister of West Kirby (Wirral Unitarians).

Richard Merritt. Although with a background as choirboy, organist and choirmaster in the Anglican church, Richard is now Chairman of Wirral Unitarians and Secretary of the Merseyside and District Missionary Association. Originally from East Yorkshire, he has developed a strong affection for the city of Liverpool and the nearby Wirral peninsula where he has lived and worked for the last forty years. Richard is also a member of the committee managing the Nightingale Centre at Great Hucklow, A keen amateur singer, pianist, organist and clarinet player, Richard is Chair of the Unitarian Music Society.

Len W. Mooney was born and educated in the East End of London. He served as an RAF pilot in the Second World War, after which he had a successful career with the Civil Aviation Authority. Len married and settled in Liverpool in 1947 where, for more than forty years, he has been an active member of Ullet Road Church and a valued officer on various committees in the District Association of Unitarian churches.

Rev Daphne M. Roberts - a Londoner. Following three years study at Unitarian College, Manchester as a mature student, where I started to learn the pitfalls of ministry, to seven years at Dob Lane Chapel in Failsworth. Here they, in their wisdom, more or less finished the job off. Thank you, folks! Finally seventeen years at Gateacre, a beautiful Queen Anne Chapel, once set in fields amongst farm houses. Here it was I found out what a wonderful heritage is to be found in Liverpool and its environs, with many thanks to those Unitarians, and others, who brought it about. Enjoy the book.

Rev Dr David Steers was born in Liverpool and educated at the Liverpool Blue Coat School and the universities of Oxford, Manchester and Glasgow. He is married to Sue and they have four children. He has been minister of the Non-Subscribing Presbyterian Churches of Downpatrick, Ballee and Clough in co. Down Northern Ireland since 2003. He is chaplain to Stranmillis University College, Belfast and the editor of the *Transactions of the Unitarian Historical Society* and *Faith and Freedom*.

Philip Waldron was born in Liverpool. He left school with no qualifications and began his working life in the field of industrial paint spraying and shot blasting, after eight years of working in this industry, he worked with the elderly and those who suffered with Multiple Sclerosis. During this time period, he got involved with a theatre company based in Southport Arts Centre. Returning to education he attended Liverpool Community College and then Bishop Grosseteste University, in Lincoln. He then worked for the Criminal Records Bureau at the same time he ran his theatre company 'Candlelight Theatre'. Throughout this time, he got involved with the community at Gateacre Chapel, becoming an active member and eventually a trustee and building manager. Presently he works as the site-manager for Ullet Road Unitarian Church and is a student minister at Unitarian College Manchester. Philip and his wife were married in Gateacre Chapel in 2010.